This book belongs to

_____

CHRISTMAS GIFTS of GOOD TASTE

ISBN: 0-8487-2717-7
ISSN: 1534-7788
Printed in the United States of America
First Printing 2003

OXMOOR HOUSE, INC.
Editor-in-Chief: Nancy Fitzpatrick Wyatt
Executive Editor: Susan Carlisle Payne
Art Director: Cynthia R. Cooper
Copy Chief: Allison Long Lowery

Christmas Gifts of Good Taste
Editors: Lauren Brooks, Leah Marlett, Susan Ray
Editorial Assistant: McCharen Pratt, Dawn Russell
Senior Photographer: Jim Bathie
Photographer: Brit Huckabay
Senior Photo Stylist: Kay E. Clarke
Photo Stylist: Ashley Wyatt
Illustrator: Kelly Davis
Director, Test Kitchens: Elizabeth Tyler Luckett
Assistant Director, Test Kitchens: Julie Christopher
Recipe Editor: Gayle Hays Sadler
Test Kitchens Staff: Kristi Carter, Nicole Faber, Jan A. Smith,
    Elise Weis, Kelley Self Wilton
Publishing Systems Administrator: Rick Tucker
Director of Production: Phillip Lee
Production Manager: Theresa L. Beste
Production Assistant: Faye Porter Bonner

Contributors:
Copy Editor: Adrienne S. Davis
Designer and Photo Stylist: Connie Formby
Indexer: Mary Ann Laurens

CHRISTMAS GIFTS of GOOD TASTE

With more than 200 great ideas for holiday gift giving, you're certain to find something for everyone on your Christmas list this year! Looking for great teacher gifts? Try the **Spiced Apple-Oatmeal Cookies** packaged in the **Blackboard Gift Bag** on page 70. Those nibblers on your list won't be able to resist the **Cracker Snackers** wrapped in a beribboned canister on page 91. And everyone will love the **Peppermint Fudge** delivered in a painted pencil box on page 124.

All of the recipes inside come complete with simple wrapping ideas. In fact, many of the packaging suggestions are so easy that no formal instructions are even needed! In many cases, the photographs show all you need to know to re-create the gift wrapping.

We hope this volume chock-full of handmade pleasures helps you create your most memorable Christmas ever.

The Editors

Oxmoor
House®

TABLE OF CONTENTS

PEANUTTY POPCORN

Who could resist popcorn coated in thick caramel and tossed with peanuts, peanut butter candy pieces, and golden raisins? It's a treat for children and adults who crave something sweet and salty. The burlap sack is the perfect size to reach in and grab a bite!

NUTTY TOFFEE POPCORN

10	cups popped popcorn
1	cup honey roasted peanuts
1	package (7.4 ounces) candy-coated peanut butter pieces
1	cup golden raisins
2⅔	cups sugar
1½	cups butter, cut into pieces
⅔	cup packed brown sugar
½	cup water
½	teaspoon salt
1	tablespoon vanilla extract

Grease a large baking sheet. Set aside.

Combine popcorn, peanuts, peanut butter pieces, and raisins in a large bowl, tossing well.

Combine sugar, butter, brown sugar, water, and salt in a 4-quart heavy saucepan. Stirring constantly, cook over medium-high heat until mixture comes to a boil. Using a pastry brush dipped in hot water, wash down any sugar crystals on sides of pan. Attach a candy thermometer to pan, making sure thermometer does not touch bottom of pan. Stirring occasionally, cook until thermometer reaches approximately 300 degrees. Remove from heat; stir in vanilla.

Gradually pour hot toffee mixture over popcorn mixture, stirring until thoroughly coated. Spread popcorn mixture onto prepared baking sheet. Flatten to ¾-inch thickness using a piece of waxed paper. Cool completely.

Break into bite-size pieces. Store in an airtight container up to 2 weeks.

Yield: about 16 cups popcorn

BURLAP BAG

You will need brown burlap, thread to match, white cardstock, black permanent fine-point marker, tan embroidery floss, embroidery needle, cellophane bag, and 1½ yds. of 1½"w sheer ribbon.

Refer to Embroidery Stitches, page 155, before beginning project.

1. Cut an 11" x 30" rectangle from burlap. Fold in half and stitch sides to make burlap bag. Turn bag right side out.
2. Referring to photo, fold top edges of burlap bag down.
3. Cut a 1½" x 2¼" rectangle from white cardstock to make label. Round corners of label.
4. Using marker, write recipe name on label. Use six strands of tan floss and embroidery needle to work *Running Stitches* along side edges of label to stitch to burlap bag.
5. Pour popcorn in cellophane bag and place inside burlap bag.
6. Tie length of ribbon around burlap bag and into a bow.

A TRADITIONAL FAVORITE

*S*hare *a little slice of heaven this Christmas by giving this tender and moist pound cake to a friend. Rhinestones outlined with gold glitter paint give this cake plate extra sparkle.*

CREAM CHEESE POUND CAKE

1½   cups butter, softened
1   package (8 ounces) cream
       cheese, softened
3   cups sugar
7   eggs
3   cups all-purpose flour
¼   teaspoon salt
2   teaspoons vanilla extract
Sifted confectioners sugar
      (optional)

Preheat oven to 325 degrees.

In a large bowl, beat butter and cream cheese at medium speed of an electric mixer about 2 minutes or until soft and creamy. Gradually add sugar, beating 2 minutes. Add eggs, one at a time, beating just until yellow disappears after each addition.

In a large bowl, combine flour and salt. Gradually add flour mixture to butter mixture, beating at low speed just until blended after each addition. Stir in vanilla.

Pour batter into a greased and floured 12-cup Bundt pan. Gently swirl a knife through batter to remove air pockets.

Bake 1 hour and 27 minutes or until a toothpick inserted in center comes out clean. Cool in pan on a wire rack 10 to 15 minutes; remove from pan, and let cool completely on wire rack. Dust with sifted confectioners sugar, if desired.

Yield: one 10-inch cake

Note: Wipe the charger plate clean with a damp paper towel. Washing the plate under water may cause the glue and rhinestones to come off.

ELEGANT CHOCOLATE CONFECTIONS

*T*he ever popular combination of strawberries and chocolate is showcased in these rich and decadent truffles. For a quick gift, place truffles in an inexpensive papier mâché or wooden box and tie with a ribbon.

STRAWBERRY-CHOCOLATE TRUFFLES

¼   cup strawberry all-fruit spread
¾   cup whipping cream
4   bars (7 ounces each) milk chocolate, coarsely chopped
1½ teaspoons vanilla extract
1   cup finely chopped almonds, toasted

In a small saucepan over medium heat, bring strawberry spread and whipping cream to a boil. Remove from heat; let cool slightly.

Melt chocolate in a heavy saucepan over low heat. Stir in strawberry mixture. Add vanilla; stir well.

Line an ungreased 9-inch square baking pan with plastic wrap, extending wrap over sides of pan. Pour chocolate mixture into prepared baking pan. Cover with plastic wrap and chill 8 hours.

Using plastic wrap, lift chilled chocolate mixture from baking pan. Using a hot knife, cut chocolate into 64 squares. Shape each square into a ball; roll in chopped almonds. Store truffles in an airtight container in the refrigerator until ready to serve. Serve at room temperature.
Yield: about 64 truffles

Note: Chill chocolate in refrigerator during rolling process, if necessary.

WINTER WARM-UP

Nothing will warm you up faster on a brisk evening than a bowl of our steaming hot soup full of vegetable goodness and accompanied by crunchy bagel croutons. The soup and croutons are packaged in coordinating containers complete with ribbons and tags, ready for delivery.

BAGEL CROUTONS

1   package bagels (we used Thomas' Everything Bagels)
4   tablespoons butter, softened
2   teaspoons garlic powder

Preheat oven to 375 degrees.
Cut bagels in half horizontally and spread with butter; sprinkle with garlic powder. Cut bagel halves into ½" cubes. Place on a greased baking sheet and bake 15 minutes or until crisp and dry.
Yield: about 5 cups croutons

STAR BAG

You will need tracing paper, gold paper, craft glue, maroon paper bag, resealable plastic bag, decorative-edge craft scissors, maroon paper, gold permanent fine-point marker, double-sided tape, hole punch, and 20" of 1¼"w wired ribbon.

1. Trace star pattern, page 139, onto tracing paper; cut out. Transfer star pattern to gold paper; cut out. Center and adhere star to front of paper bag using craft glue.
2. Place croutons in plastic bag and place inside paper bag. Cut top edge of paper bag using craft scissors.

3. Fold top edge of paper bag down 1½". Cut a 1" x 5" rectangle from gold paper using decorative-edge craft scissors. Referring to photo, glue rectangle to paper bag under fold so gold edge extends slightly.
4. Cut a 2¼" x 3" rectangle from gold paper. Cut a 2" x 2¾" rectangle from maroon paper. Center and glue maroon rectangle to gold rectangle to make label. Using marker, write recipe name and draw stars on label. Adhere label to front of paper bag using double-sided tape.
5. Punch two holes at top of paper bag. Thread ribbon through holes and tie into a knot.

ITALIAN VEGETABLE SOUP

2   medium leeks
2   tablespoons olive oil
1   package (10 ounces) match-stick cut carrots, about 3 cups
2   medium zucchini, cut in half lengthwise and sliced
1   can (28 ounces) diced tomatoes, undrained
1   can (15 ounces) dark red kidney beans, drained
4   cans (14 ounces) ready-to-serve chicken broth
1   teaspoon dried Italian seasoning
½   teaspoon salt
3   cloves garlic, minced (about 1 tablespoon)
¼   teaspoon pepper
¾   cup macaroni
⅓   cup grated Parmesan cheese
¼   cup chopped fresh parsley
Bagel Croutons (at left)

Remove roots, tough outer leaves, and tops from leeks, leaving 4 inches of dark leaves. Split leeks in half lengthwise; wash well. Slice leeks thinly and set aside.
Heat oil over medium-high heat in a large Dutch oven; add leeks and carrots and sauté 7 minutes or until tender.
Stir in zucchini, tomato, kidney beans, broth, seasoning, salt, garlic, and pepper; stir well. Bring mixture to a boil; add pasta. Reduce heat and simmer 10 to 12 minutes or until pasta is tender. Sprinkle with Parmesan cheese and parsley. To serve, ladle soup into individual soup bowls. Top with Bagel Croutons.
Yield: about 14 cups soup

FABRIC-COVERED
SOUP TUREEN

You will need fabric, container with lid, rubber band, 3 yds. of 1¼"w wired ribbon, gold paper, maroon paper, craft glue, gold permanent fine-point marker, hole punch, and gold thread.

Allow glue to dry after each application.

1. Cut a 36" dia. circle from fabric.

Pour soup into container and replace lid. Set container in center of fabric circle.

2. Pull fabric up around container and gather at top. Secure ends with rubber band.

3. Tuck ends into center so only right side of fabric shows.

4. Following *Making a Bow,* page 152, tie ribbon into a multi-looped bow around rubber band.

5. Cut a 3" x 4¼" rectangle from gold paper. Cut a 3" x 3¾" rectangle from maroon paper. Center and glue maroon rectangle to gold rectangle. Fold in half to make gift tag.

6. Referring to photo and using marker, write greeting and draw stars on tag. Punch hole in tag through fold and thread onto gold thread. Tie thread to bow.

15

CHUNKY CHOCOLATE PIE, OH MY!

Overflowing with walnuts, chocolate, and dates, this mouth-watering pie in a flaky crust will beckon guests to the dessert table. The pastry leaf cutouts make it a showstopper. For an easy yet regal touch, glue rhinestones around the pie plate lid.

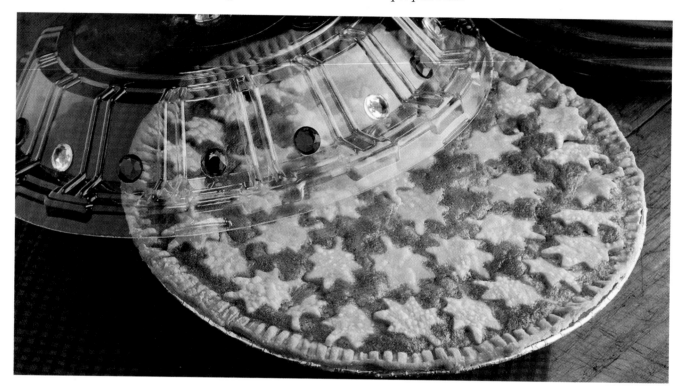

CHOCOLATE-DATE-WALNUT PIE

1	package (15 ounces) refrigerated pie crusts, at room temperature
¾	cup light corn syrup
4	eggs
2	teaspoons vanilla extract
1	cup packed brown sugar
1	teaspoon all-purpose flour
½	teaspoon salt
1	cup chopped walnuts
¾	cup semisweet chocolate chips
½	cup chopped dates

Preheat oven to 350 degrees. Roll 1 pie crust to ⅛-inch thickness on a lightly floured surface. Place in 9-inch disposable pie plate. Roll remaining pie crust to ⅛-inch thickness; cut into small leaves and stems, using a cookie cutter or small knife.

Combine corn syrup, eggs, and vanilla in large bowl. Combine brown sugar, flour, and salt; add to corn syrup mixture, stirring until well blended. Stir in walnuts.

Sprinkle chocolate chips and dates evenly in pastry shell. Pour walnut mixture over chocolate and dates. Arrange reserved pastry cutouts over filling. Bake 41 minutes or until filling is set. Cover edges with aluminum foil after 30 minutes to prevent overbrowning, if needed. Cool completely.
Yield: one 9-inch pie

*T*hick potato chips or assorted vegetables are a must for scooping up this creamy onion-packed dip. You might think pistachios sound like an out-of-place ingredient, but they add a bit of crunch to this otherwise smooth dip. Personalize a disposable container with dimensional paint and ribbon.

GOLDEN ONION DIP

- 2 large sweet onions, chopped (about 5½ cups)
- 2 tablespoons butter, melted
- ½ cup chicken broth
- 1 package (8 ounces) cream cheese, softened
- 1 cup mayonnaise
- ½ cup coarsely chopped pistachios, toasted

Whole pistachios to garnish

Cook onion in butter in a large nonstick skillet over medium-high heat, stirring constantly, until onion is tender. Add chicken broth; bring to a boil. Cook over medium-high heat 15 minutes or until onion is golden, stirring frequently. Remove from heat, and let cool completely.

Beat cream cheese at medium speed of an electric mixer until creamy. Add mayonnaise, beating until smooth. Stir in onion mixture and chopped pistachios. Cover and chill. Garnish, if desired. Serve with ruffled potato chips, assorted fresh vegetables, or Melba rounds. *Yield:* about 4 cups dip

LUSCIOUS LEMON PIE

This tangy lemon pie adds a little sunshine to a winter day. It can be served warm, cold, or at room temperature and crowned with a scoop of vanilla ice cream. Simply wrap the pie in a large tea towel, tie with yellow ribbon, and add a handmade, cross-stitched ornament, if desired.

LEMON SLICE CUSTARD PIE

3   small thin-skinned lemons
1¾   cups sugar
1½   packages (15 ounces each) refrigerated pie crusts, at room temperature
3   tablespoons all-purpose flour
¼   teaspoon salt
¼   cup butter, melted
4   eggs, lightly beaten
1   tablespoon lemon juice
1   egg white
1   teaspoon sugar

Freeze lemons 2 hours. Cut lemons into quarters lengthwise. Using a sharp knife, trim ends and cut lemon quarters crosswise into ⅛-inch wedges. Remove and discard seeds.

In a medium bowl, combine lemon slices and 1¾ cups sugar. Let stand 2 hours.

Preheat oven to 400 degrees.

Place 1 pie crust in a 9-inch pie plate and set aside.

In a large bowl, combine flour and salt; whisk in butter, eggs, and lemon juice. Stir in lemon slice mixture. Spoon into crust.

Place remaining crust over filling; use sharp knife to trim both edges of dough. Seal and crimp edges. Cut lemon wedge shapes from remaining pie crust to place on top of pie. Lightly whisk egg white. Brush crust with egg white; sprinkle 1 teaspoon sugar over crust. Cut slits around center of pie. Bake 15 minutes. Reduce heat to 350 degrees and bake 25 minutes or until crust is golden brown, covering edges with aluminum foil to prevent overbrowning, if necessary. Cool pie on a wire rack.
Yield: about 8 servings

CROSS-STITCHED ORNAMENT

You will need white Aida (14 ct); embroidery floss (see color key, page 140); embroidery needle; orange, pink, and green felt; and thread to match.

Refer to Cross Stitch, page 154, and Embroidery Stitches, page 155, before beginning project.

1. Cut a 5" square piece of Aida and turn on point. Using three strands of floss for *Cross Stitches* and one strand of floss for *Backstitches* and *French Knots*, center and stitch design, page 140, on Aida.
2. Turn edges of Aida under and press to finish raw edges.
3. Cut a 3¾" square of orange felt. Referring to photo, cut points around edges of square. Cut a 4" square of pink felt. Referring to photo, cut points around edges of square. Cut a 4¾" square of green felt. Referring to photo, cut points around edges of square.
4. Referring to photo, turn felt squares on point and stack with Aida on top. Stitch around folded edges of Aida and through all three layers of felt to make ornament.
5. Cut a ¾" x 6" rectangle from orange felt. Fold rectangle in half and stitch ends to back side of ornament to make hanger.

SWEET MORNING TREAT

Hidden inside these savory muffins is a layer of maple pecan sweetness that will tantalize your taste buds with each bite. Colored wooden beads add flair to a simple basket that's lined with a festive cloth to keep the muffins warm for delivery.

PECAN CORN MUFFINS

⅔   cup finely chopped pecans
3   tablespoons maple syrup
1⅓   cups all-purpose flour
1   cup yellow cornmeal
1   tablespoon sugar
2½   teaspoons baking
        powder
½   teaspoon baking soda
½   teaspoon salt
1¼   cups buttermilk
⅓   cup butter, melted
1   egg, beaten
1   egg yolk

Preheat oven to 375 degrees.

In a small bowl, combine pecans and maple syrup; stir well and set aside. Grease muffin pans.

In a large bowl, combine flour, cornmeal, sugar, baking powder, baking soda, and salt; make a well in center of flour mixture.

Combine buttermilk, butter, egg, and egg yolk; stir well. Add to flour mixture, stirring just until moistened. Spoon about 2 tablespoons batter into greased muffin pans. Spoon about 1 tablespoon reserved pecan mixture over batter. Top pecan mixture with remaining batter.

Bake 25 minutes or until lightly browned. Remove from pans immediately; transfer to a wire rack to cool 10 minutes before serving.

Yield: about 1 dozen muffins

WOODEN BEAD BASKET AND NAPKIN

You will need a wooden basket with side handles; white, red, and green acrylic paints; ½" solid wooden beads; ½" wooden beads with holes; hot glue gun; red linen napkin; thread to match napkin; decorative paper; red vellum; glue stick; silver paint pen; hole punch; and 25" of 1½"w sheer ribbon.

Allow paint to dry after each application.

1. Paint basket using white paint. Paint 8 solid wooden beads using red paint. Paint 8 solid wooden beads and 4 wooden beads with holes using green paint.
2. Using hot glue gun and referring to photo, glue solid wooden beads along top edge of basket, alternating red and green beads and leaving approximately ½" between each bead.
3. Stitch remaining four green beads with holes to each corner of napkin.
4. Cut a 2½" x 3½" rectangle from decorative paper. Cut a 2" x 3" rectangle from red vellum. Center and adhere red vellum rectangle to decorative paper rectangle using glue stick to make gift tag. Write recipe name on tag using paint pen.
5. Punch hole in top of tag and thread onto ribbon. Tie ribbon around basket handle and into a bow. Thread ornament onto ribbon, if desired.

*B*ring the flavor of Italy to a friend's table with this versatile blend that can be added to a favorite pasta sauce or used to make delicious Italian Crostini. Place the blend in a resealable plastic bag before setting it in a paper sack. For an elegant twist on a simple packaging idea, fold ribbon into a "V" shape and staple it to the paper sack. Don't forget to include the crostini recipe card.

TASTE OF TUSCANY

¼   cup dried sage
¼   cup dried rosemary
1   teaspoon salt
½   teaspoon black peppercorns

Place all ingredients in a mini food processor or coffee grinder; process until finely ground.
Yield: about ½ cup mix

Italian Crostini

Slice a 1-pound French baguette into ½-inch-thick slices. Brush each slice with olive oil, and rub with a garlic clove. Combine 4 ounces softened goat cheese or cream cheese and 1 teaspoon Taste of Tuscany; spread over slices. Top with roasted red pepper strips. Broil until lightly browned. Serve immediately.

FESTIVE COOKIES

*R*ed and green maraschino cherries dot these chunky cookies that have bits of crunch and flavor throughout. Package these colorful cookies in a wrapped box and watch them vanish in the twinkling of an eye.

VANILLA CHERRY COOKIES

1   jar (6 ounces) red maraschino cherries, drained
1   jar (6 ounces) green maraschino cherries, drained
½   cup butter, softened
½   cup vegetable shortening
1   package (3 ounces) cream cheese, softened
1   cup sugar
1   cup firmly packed brown sugar
2   eggs
1½ teaspoons vanilla extract
2   cups all-purpose flour
1   teaspoon baking powder
½   teaspoon salt
1   cup quick-cooking oats, uncooked
1   cup crispy rice cereal
1   cup chopped pecans
1   cup flaked coconut
1   package (12 ounces) premier white chips

Preheat oven to 350 degrees. Chop cherries; drain on paper towels. Set aside. In a large bowl, cream butter, shortening, and cream cheese at medium speed of an electric mixer until fluffy; add sugars, beating well. Add eggs and vanilla; beat until smooth.

In a medium bowl, combine flour, baking powder, and salt. Add dry ingredients to creamed mixture; stir until a soft dough forms. Stir in cherries, oats, cereal, pecans, coconut, and white chips.

Drop by tablespoonfuls 2 inches apart onto lightly greased baking sheets. Bake 12 minutes or until lightly browned. Let cookies stand on baking sheets 1 minute; transfer cookies to a wire rack to cool.

Yield: about 4 dozen cookies

PUCKER UP FOR CAKE

Share slices of this moist cake dappled with chocolate chips and lemon rind at an intimate tea party among friends. A painted plate with matching server will showcase the cake nicely.

CHOCOLATE CHIP-LEMON CAKE

½ cup butter, softened
1 cup sugar, divided
2 eggs
1⅔ cups all-purpose flour
1 teaspoon baking powder
½ teaspoon baking soda
½ teaspoon salt
½ cup ground toasted almonds
1 teaspoon grated lemon zest
1 carton (8 ounces) sour cream
¾ cup semisweet chocolate mini chips
1 teaspoon vanilla extract
¼ teaspoon lemon extract
3 tablespoons frozen lemonade concentrate, thawed
2 tablespoons water

Preheat oven to 350 degrees.

In a large bowl, beat butter at medium speed of an electric mixer until fluffy. Gradually add ⅔ cup sugar; beat well. Add eggs, 1 at a time, beating well after each addition.

In a small bowl, combine flour, baking powder, baking soda, salt, almonds, and lemon zest; add to creamed mixture alternately with sour cream, beginning and ending with flour mixture. Mix after each addition. Stir in mini chips and extracts. Spoon batter into a greased and floured 6-cup Bundt pan. Bake 35 to 40 minutes or until a toothpick inserted in center comes out clean. While cake is baking, combine remaining ⅓ cup sugar, lemonade concentrate, and water in a saucepan. Bring to a boil; reduce heat, and simmer 1 minute. Cool cake 10 minutes in pan; remove from pan. Pour glaze over.

Yield: one 7½-inch cake

Note: When glazing cake, place cake on a wire rack with a pan underneath to catch drips.

PAINTED CAKE PLATE AND WIRE SERVER

You will need a 12" dia. glass cake plate; red, green, and gold enamel glass paints; paintbrush; stainless steel cake server; ½ yd. each of red, green, and gold 16-gauge craft wire; needle-nose pliers; red vellum; gold paint pen; and hole punch.

Allow paint to dry after each application.

1. Clean and prepare bottom surface of cake plate according to manufacturer's instructions for using glass paint.
2. Referring to photo and using red and green enamel paints, paint stripes around bottom edge of cake plate, alternating colors. Using gold enamel paint, paint gold stripe between red and green stripes.
3. Using pliers and referring to photo, wrap red craft wire around handle of cake server, looping sharp ends of wire under. Repeat with gold and green craft wire.
4. Cut a 2" x 3" rectangle from vellum to make gift tag. Using paint pen, write recipe name on tag. Punch hole in corner of tag and thread onto end of wire on cake server.

25

*P*otato sticks provide a salty crunch to these otherwise sweet treats that contain only three ingredients. For a rustic presentation use a sprig of fresh rosemary to form a wreath on a brown bag and accentuate the charming circle with a pinecone and jute bow.

BUTTERSCOTCH DROPS

1	package (6 ounces) butterscotch chips
1	cup dry-roasted peanuts
1	cup shoestring potato sticks, broken into pieces

Melt chips in a saucepan over low heat. Stir in peanuts and potato sticks. Drop by tablespoonfuls onto waxed paper, and cool completely.
Yield: about 2½ dozen candies

WREATH BAG

You will need hole punch, paper bag, jute twine, sprigs of rosemary, craft wire, and small pinecone.

1. Punch two holes in front of bag, 2" from top and spaced about 1½" apart.
2. Cut a 6" length of jute twine. Thread length of jute twine through holes in bag, beginning at back of bag and pulling through front.
3. Wire rosemary sprigs together to

form wreath. Attach wreath to bag using jute twine.
4. Following *Making a Bow,* page 152, cut a 32" length of jute twine and tie twine around

rosemary wreath into multi-looped bow.
5. Wrap a small length of craft wire around bottom of pinecone and attach to center of bow.

MADE-WITH-LOVE LOAF

Flavored with dried apricots and sweetened orange juice, this tasty bread is sure to be a Christmas favorite. Tuck the bread into a purchased resealable bag tied with a ribbon for a thoughtful gift for family and friends.

APRICOT-PECAN BREAD

2½	cups dried apricots, chopped
1	cup chopped pecans
4	cups all-purpose flour, divided
¼	cup butter, softened
2	cups sugar
2	eggs
1	tablespoon plus 1 teaspoon baking powder
½	teaspoon baking soda
½	teaspoon salt
1½	cups orange juice

Preheat oven to 350 degrees.

Combine chopped apricots and warm water to cover in a large bowl; let stand 30 minutes. Drain apricots. Stir in pecans and ½ cup flour; set aside.

In a large bowl, beat butter at medium speed with an electric mixer 2 minutes or until fluffy; gradually add sugar, beating well. Add eggs, one at a time, beating after each addition.

In a large bowl, combine remaining 3½ cups flour, baking powder, soda, and salt. Add to creamed mixture alternately with orange juice, beginning and ending with flour mixture. Stir in apricot mixture. Spoon into 2 greased and floured 8 x 4-inch loafpans; let stand at room temperature 20 minutes. Bake 1 hour or until a toothpick inserted in center comes out clean. Cool in pans on wire rack 10 to 15 minutes; remove from pans, and cool completely on a wire rack.
Yield: 2 loaves

SAVORY GREEK TREATS

Spruce up a holiday evening by serving these bite-size Greek Olive Cups. They can be filled, placed in trays, and frozen until ready to use. To present them as a gift, wrap in decorated cardboard sleeves and include reheating instructions.

GREEK OLIVE CUPS

1	cup (4 ounces) shredded Cheddar cheese
½	cup chopped pimento-stuffed olives or other green olives
½	cup kalamata olives, pitted and chopped
⅓	cup chopped pecans, toasted
⅓	cup pine nuts, toasted
2½	tablespoons mayonnaise
2	packages (2.1 ounces each) frozen mini phyllo shells

Preheat oven to 375 degrees. Combine Cheddar cheese, green olives, kalamata olives, pecans, pine nuts, and mayonnaise. Remove phyllo shells from packages, leaving them in trays.

Spoon 1 heaping teaspoon olive mixture into each phyllo shell. Remove from trays, and place cups on an ungreased baking sheet. Bake 12 to 15 minutes or until thoroughly heated. Serve immediately.
Yield: about 30 appetizer servings

To Make Ahead: After filling cups in trays, they may be placed in heavy-duty resealable plastic bags, and frozen up to 1 month. When ready to bake, remove cups from trays and place on an ungreased baking sheet. Let cups stand 10 minutes before baking. Bake as directed in recipe.

CORRUGATED SLEEVE

You will need corrugated cardboard, hole punch, 2½ yds. of 1½"w plaid ribbon, green decorative paper, black and cream cardstock, black permanent fine-point marker, craft glue, and hot glue gun.

1. Cut a 16" x 22" piece from cardboard. Fold cardboard in half. Punch four holes along short sides, 2½" apart, through both layers. Referring to photo, punch hole in center at edge of long open side, through both layers.
2. Cut eight, 9" lengths of ribbon. Tie one ribbon length through each hole and into a knot to join layers and to form cardboard pouch.
3. Tear an 8" x 9" rectangle from green decorative paper. Tear a 5" square from black cardstock. Tear a 1½" x 3½" rectangle from cream cardstock.
4. Using marker, write recipe name on cream rectangle. Center and adhere cream rectangle to black square using craft glue. Center and adhere black square to green rectangle using craft glue to make label. Adhere label in center at top of cardboard pouch using hot glue gun.
5. Place tray of olive cups in a resealable plastic bag. Place olive cups inside cardboard pouch. Cut 12" length of ribbon. Tie ribbon through holes in center of long sides to form closure.

Greek Olive Cups

These tasty croutons can be served on top of a salad, sprinkled over a creamy soup, or used as a topping for casseroles. Wrap them in a cellophane bag with ribbons and a tag for a touch of flair.

HERBED CROUTONS

2	cups ½–inch cubed French bread

Olive-oil flavored cooking spray

½	tablespoon dried Italian seasoning
¼	teaspoon salt
¼	teaspoon pepper

Preheat oven to 400 degrees. Place bread cubes on a jelly-roll pan; lightly coat bread cubes with cooking spray. Toss bread cubes with seasoning, salt, and pepper. Bake 10 minutes or until golden. *Yield:* about 16 (¼ cup) servings

PARMESAN CROUTONS

2	cups ½-inch cubed French bread

Olive-oil flavored cooking spray

1	tablespoon shredded Parmesan cheese
¼	teaspoon salt
¼	teaspoon pepper

Preheat oven to 400 degrees. Place bread cubes on a jelly-roll pan; lightly coat bread cubes with cooking spray. Toss bread cubes with cheese, salt, and pepper. Bake 10 minutes or until golden. *Yield:* about 16 (¼ cup) servings

CELLOPHANE BAG

You will need cellophane bag, 25" of ½"w ribbon, green handmade paper, and black permanent fine-point marker.

1. Pour croutons in cellophane bag.

2. Tie ribbon around cellophane bag and into a bow.

3. Transfer tree pattern, page 139, to green handmade paper; cut out to make gift tag. Write recipe name on tag using marker. Cut slit in tag, and thread onto ribbon.

SANTA'S FAVORITE SNACK

*P*opcorn and chocolate team up to provide the perfect sweet and salty flavor combo. A stenciled tin holds plenty of this chocolatey treat, sure to become a holiday favorite among children and adults alike.

DELICIOUS CHOCOLATE POPCORN

12   cups popped popcorn
1   cup sugar
⅔   cup dark corn syrup
2   tablespoons butter
1   package (6 ounces) semisweet chocolate chips
1   teaspoon vanilla extract

Preheat oven to 250 degrees. Place popcorn on a lightly greased roasting pan; set aside.

Bring sugar, syrup, and butter to a boil in a saucepan over medium heat, stirring constantly. Remove from heat; add chocolate chips and vanilla, stirring until melted.

Drizzle chocolate mixture over popcorn, stirring to coat.

Bake 1 hour, stirring occasionally. Transfer popcorn to a waxed paper-lined pan to cool, stirring occasionally. Store in an airtight container.
Yield: about 12 cups popcorn

HOLLY TIN

You will need a tin with lid, tan and red spray paints, tracing paper, craft sponge, green and red

acrylic paints, hot glue gun, 1 yd. of ½"w plaid ribbon, brown paper, black permanent fine-point marker, hole punch, and raffia.

Refer to Painting Techniques, page 153, before beginning project. Allow paint to dry after each application.

1. Spray paint tin using tan paint. Spray paint lid of tin using red paint.
2. Trace holly leaf pattern, page 139, onto tracing paper; cut out. Transfer holly leaf pattern to craft sponge; cut out.
3. Follow *Sponge Painting* to paint holly leaves around sides of tin using green paint.
4. Paint berries onto tin using red paint.
5. Referring to photo and using hot glue gun, adhere ribbon around side of lid.
6. Cut 2¼" x 4¼" rectangle from brown paper. Fold in half to make gift tag. Using marker, write greeting on tag. Punch hole in tag through fold.
7. Pour popcorn in tin.
8. Cut length of raffia. Thread tag onto length of raffia and tie around tin.

CHOCO-MINT INDULGENCE

*T*hree ingredients are all it takes to make a rich brownie mint pie that's a snap to prepare. Place the pie in a clever carrier and give to a chocolate mint lover. Glue holly leaves and berries to the pie carrier for holiday pizzazz.

BROWNIE MINT PIE

1   package (4.6 ounces)
    chocolate mints
1   package (10.25 ounces)
    brownie mix
1   unbaked 9-inch pie crust

Preheat oven to 350 degrees.
Chop chocolate mints. Prepare brownie mix according to package directions; stir chopped mints into brownie batter. Pour into pie crust.
Bake 45 minutes or until a toothpick inserted in center of pie comes out clean; cool slightly.
Yield: one 9-inch pie

MERRY MERINGUES

*T*he coffee lovers on your list will be overjoyed to receive a hand-painted mug overflowing with chocolate-dipped coffee confections. Bite-size drops of coffee meringue are baked golden and crisp, then dipped in chocolate and nuts for a sweet finish. They taste great alongside a steaming mug of coffee.

CHOCOLATE-DIPPED COFFEE DROPS

3	egg whites
¼	teaspoon cream of tartar
1	tablespoon instant coffee granules
1	cup sugar
½	teaspoon vanilla extract
½	cup chopped walnuts
4	squares (2 ounces each) chocolate candy coating, melted
1	cup finely chopped walnuts, toasted

Preheat oven to 225 degrees.

Beat egg whites, cream of tartar, and coffee granules at high speed of an electric mixer just until foamy. Add sugar, 1 tablespoon at a time, beating until stiff peaks form and sugar dissolves (2 to 4 minutes). Stir in vanilla and ½ cup chopped walnuts.

Drop by tablespoonfuls onto parchment paper-lined baking sheets.

Bake 1 hour and 15 minutes. Turn oven off, and leave cookies in oven 2 hours.

Dip bottom of each cookie in melted coating, and press into 1

cup toasted walnuts. Place on waxed paper until dry.

Yield: about 3 dozen meringues

SNOWFLAKE MUG

You will need a large coffee mug, tracing paper, transfer paper, white enamel ceramic paint with pointed-tip applicator, decorative paper, hole punch, silver paint pen, silver ribbon, and cellophane bag.

Allow paint to dry after each application.

1. Trace snowflake pattern, page 141, onto tracing paper. Transfer snowflake pattern onto one side of mug.

2. Using white ceramic paint with applicator, paint over snowflake pattern using thin bead of paint. Place mug on its side to let paint dry completely.

3. Repeat Steps 1 and 2 for opposite side of mug, if desired.

4. Using white ceramic paint with applicator and referring to photo, paint small dots around top rim and bottom edge of cup.

5. Cut a 2" x 4" rectangle from decorative paper to make gift tag. Punch a hole in corner of tag. Using silver paint pen, write recipe name on tag.

6. Cut a 10" length of ribbon. Thread tag onto ribbon.

7. Place meringues in cellophane bag and tie bag with ribbon. Place cellophane bag inside coffee mug.

MARVELOUS MUFFINS

The irresistible aroma of apples and cinnamon baked into a warm muffin would please even Scrooge himself. Tuck the muffins into a lined basket and adorn with decorative apples and a tag for a gift from the heart.

CHUNKY-FRIED APPLE MUFFINS

2	cups all-purpose flour
1	tablespoon baking powder
¼	teaspoon salt
¼	cup sugar
1	teaspoon ground cinnamon
1	egg
½	cup milk
¼	cup molasses
¼	cup vegetable oil
1	cup finely chopped canned fried apples
3	tablespoons all-purpose flour
3	tablespoons sugar
¼	teaspoon ground cinnamon
1½	tablespoons butter

Preheat oven to 400 degrees.

In a large bowl, combine 2 cups flour, baking powder, salt, ¼ cup sugar, and 1 teaspoon cinnamon; make a well in center of mixture. Combine egg, milk, molasses, and oil; add to dry ingredients. Stir just until moistened; fold in fried apple.

Combine 3 tablespoons flour, 3 tablespoons sugar, and ¼ teaspoon cinnamon in a small bowl; using a pastry blender or 2 knives, cut in butter until mixture resembles coarse meal.

Fill greased muffin cups about three-fourths full. Sprinkle streusel mixture evenly over batter in each cup. Bake 15 to 16 minutes or until a toothpick inserted in center of muffin comes out clean. Remove from pan and cool on a wire rack. Store in an airtight container.
Yield: about 1 dozen muffins

APPLE BASKET

You will need hot glue gun, artificial apples and leaves, basket with handle, apple plaid decorative paper, brown paper, glue stick, black permanent fine-point marker, hole punch, jute twine, and cloth napkin.

Allow glue to dry after each application.

1. Referring to photo and using hot glue gun, adhere apples and leaves to each side of basket handle.
2. Cut a 2½" x 4" rectangle from apple plaid decorative paper. Cut a 2" x 3" rectangle from brown paper. Using glue stick, center and adhere brown rectangle to decorative rectangle to make gift tag. Using marker, write recipe name on tag.
3. Punch hole in tag and thread onto length of jute twine. Tie twine around basket handle and into a knot. Trim ends of twine.
4. Place cloth napkin and muffins inside basket.

SOUP THAT SATISFIES

A *container filled with our creamy Spinach-and-Tomato Soup will be warmly received this holiday, especially when given with an assortment of crackers. Make a festive package for the ensemble by adorning a paper bag with a ribbon wreath.*

SPINACH-AND-TOMATO SOUP

1	large onion, thinly sliced and separated into rings
3	tablespoons butter, melted
3	cups chicken broth, divided
2	cups half-and-half
3	tablespoons all-purpose flour
1	package (10 ounces) fresh spinach, chopped
3	medium tomatoes, seeded and chopped
½	teaspoon salt
¼	teaspoon pepper
¼	teaspoon dried dillweed

Sauté onion in butter in a large Dutch oven until tender. Stir in 2½ cups chicken broth and half-and-half. Bring just to a simmer; simmer 10 minutes. Combine remaining ½ cup chicken broth and flour, stirring until smooth. Add to Dutch oven; stir well. Cook over medium heat, stirring constantly, until mixture is slightly thickened.

Stir in spinach, tomatoes, salt, pepper, and dillweed. Cook 5 minutes or until spinach wilts and soup is thoroughly heated.
Yield: about 8 cups soup

RIBBON-WREATH BAG

You will need a large paper bag with handles, 3 yds. of 1" green grosgrain ribbon, glue, hole punch, ½ yd. of ½" red grosgrain ribbon, red cardstock, silver paint pen, and 2½-quart airtight container.

1. Mark a 5" dia. circle in center of one side of bag. Cut 24 (3") lengths of green ribbon. Referring to photo, glue each ribbon length around circle.
2. Punch two holes at top of bag inside ribbon circle. Referring to photo, thread red ribbon through holes and tie into bow.
3. Cut a 4" x 2" gift tag from cardstock. Cut a 4" length from green ribbon. Glue ribbon to one short edge of tag. Punch hole at ribbon end of tag. Using silver paint pen, write recipe name and serving instructions on tag.
4. Pour soup into plastic container and place inside bag. Thread another length of green ribbon through hole in tag. Tie ribbon onto bag handle and into a bow.

FESTIVE FRUIT MEDLEY

*T*his versatile fruit mix can be chopped for use in baked goods, served over pork, or poured over cream cheese and served with crackers. Package it in a cinnamon-framed bag, or use it in the Fruitcake Loaves on page 37.

DRIED FRUIT MIX

¾	cup orange essence pitted plums
½	cup dried apricots
½	cup dried apple slices
5	dried figs, halved
1	orange
1	cup dried cranberries
½	cup dried cherries
½	cup flaked coconut
¼	cup raisins
¼	cup golden raisins
½	cup brandy
½	cup honey
½	teaspoon ground cinnamon
¼	teaspoon ground cloves

Combine plums, apricots, apple slices, and figs in a bowl. Peel orange, reserving sections for another use. Cut enough rind into very thin strips to measure ¼ cup; stir ¼ cup rind, cranberries, cherries, coconut, raisins, and golden raisins into plum mixture.

Combine brandy, honey, cinnamon, and cloves in a saucepan; cook over medium heat 3 minutes or until warm. Pour over fruit mixture, stirring gently. Serve warm or at room temperature. Refrigerate in an airtight container up to one month.
Yield: about 4⅓ cups fruit mix

MIX BAG

You will need resealable plastic bag, decorative paper bag, hole punch, 12" of 1½"w sheer wired ribbon, cream-colored handmade paper, brown permanent fine-point marker, hot glue gun, and cinnamon sticks.

1. Pour mix in resealable plastic bag and place inside decorative bag.
2. Fold top of bag 1" to back. Punch two holes at top of paper bag, spaced about 1½" apart.
3. Thread length of ribbon through holes. Trim ends of ribbon diagonally.
4. Cut a 3½" x 5½" rectangle from handmade paper to make label. Using marker, write recipe name and serving suggestions on label. Using glue stick, adhere label to front of paper bag.
5. Cut two 4" lengths and two 6" lengths of cinnamon sticks. Referring to photo, hot-glue cinnamon sticks around edges of label.

LOADED LOAVES OF FRUIT

*T*his updated version of fruitcake uses nine types of dried fruit instead of the colored jellied fruits that your mom used to use. The result is an explosion of holiday taste, all packed into a wooden crate filled with excelsior and accented with a bow.

FRUITCAKE LOAVES

1	cup all-purpose flour, divided
1	cup Dried Fruit Mix, page 36
¼	cup dried apple slices
¼	cup dried cranberries
¼	cup golden raisins
3	dried figs, chopped
1	cup pecan pieces
¾	cup butter, softened
½	cup firmly packed brown sugar
2	eggs
½	teaspoon baking soda
½	teaspoon ground nutmeg
½	teaspoon ground cinnamon
½	cup light corn syrup

Preheat oven to 300 degrees.

Grease three 5¾ x 3¼-inch loafpans. Line just the bottoms of pans with parchment paper; grease paper, and set pans aside. Combine ½ cup flour, Dried Fruit Mix, remaining dried fruit, and pecans, tossing gently to coat; set aside. Beat butter at medium speed of an electric mixer until creamy. Gradually add brown sugar, beating well. Add eggs, one at a time, beating well after each addition.

Combine remaining ½ cup flour, soda, nutmeg, and cinnamon; gradually add to butter mixture, beating at low speed until blended. Add corn syrup, beating just until blended. Stir in fruit mixture; spoon into prepared pans. Bake 1 hour and 15 minutes. Cool in pans on wire rack 10 minutes; run a sharp knife around cakes to loosen from sides of pans. Remove cakes from pans,

and peel off paper. Cool completely on a wire rack.
Yield: 3 small loaves fruitcake

Note: When cutting squares of parchment paper to line the bottom of pans, cut three equal-size squares of paper and place on the bottom of an inverted pan. Holding the paper with one hand, cut the paper using the inverted pan as a guide.

ITALIAN CHEESE BITES

*H*oliday snacking doesn't get any easier than opening a jar of Marinated Mozzarella,
ready to be eaten alone or with crackers. It's a great gift for people who entertain,
as it keeps for two weeks and the longer it sits the better it tastes. Create our decorative tin
topped canister or purchase a pretty jar for gift-giving.

MARINATED MOZZARELLA

1   pound mozzarella cheese, cut into 1-inch cubes
1   jar (7 ounces) roasted red peppers, drained and cut into thin strips
2   cloves garlic, cut in half lengthwise
1¼ cups olive oil
1   tablespoon plus 1 teaspoon dried Italian seasoning
1   teaspoon dried crushed red pepper
    Fresh rosemary or thyme sprigs (optional)

Combine cheese, pepper strips, and garlic in a 1-quart jar, and set aside. Combine olive oil, Italian seasoning, and crushed red pepper. Pour over cheese mixture. Add fresh rosemary or thyme sprigs, if desired. Cover tightly and shake vigorously. Chill at least 4 hours. Drain and serve with assorted crackers. Store in refrigerator up to 2 weeks.
Yield: about 4 cups mozzarella

DECORATIVE TIN CANISTER

You will need a large glass canister with airtight lid, 1 yd. of red grosgrain ribbon, craft glue, checked decorative paper, red vellum, silver paint pen, red crafting metal, stylus tool, hole punch, and red raffia.

1. Beginning and ending at top, measure length around canister. Cut grosgrain ribbon to fit. Referring to photo and using craft glue, glue ribbon lengthwise around canister.
2. Cut a 4" square from checked paper. Cut a 2½" square from red vellum. Using silver paint pen, write recipe name on red vellum square. Center and glue red vellum square onto checked paper square. Referring to photo, center and glue label on top of ribbon and onto canister.
3. Cut a square of crafting metal to fit top of canister lid. Using stylus tool, draw swirls as desired on metal. Using craft glue, adhere metal to canister lid.
4. Cut 2" x 4" rectangles from checked paper and red vellum. Glue red vellum rectangle to wrong side of checked paper rectangle. Fold rectangle in half lengthwise with checked paper on outside to make gift tag.
5. Using silver paint pen, write serving suggestions for marinated mozzarella inside tag. Using hole punch, cut hole in corner of tag through fold.
6. Cut length of raffia ribbon. Thread tag onto raffia and tie around neck of canister and into a bow.
7. Place marinated mozzarella into canister.

CHERRIES BRING CHEER

*P*ut *a smile on someone's face by presenting this prettily packaged Cherry Fudge Cake as a Christmas surprise. It comes together in a twinkle thanks to convenience products like cake mix and cherry pie filling, must have ingredients for quick gifts.*

CHERRY FUDGE CAKE

1	package (18.25 ounces) devil's food cake mix with pudding
1	can (21 ounces) cherry pie filling
2	eggs
1	teaspoon almond extract
1	cup sugar
⅓	cup butter
⅓	cup milk
1	cup (6 ounces) semisweet chocolate chips

Preheat oven to 350 degrees.

In a bowl, combine cake mix, pie filling, eggs, and almond extract until blended. Pour into a greased and floured 13 x 9-inch pan.

Bake 30 minutes or until a toothpick inserted in center comes out clean. Cool in pan on a wire rack.

Combine sugar, butter, and milk in a small saucepan. Bring to a boil, stirring constantly; reduce heat, and simmer, stirring constantly, 1 minute. Remove from heat; stir in chocolate chips until blended. Pour over cooled cake, spreading if necessary, and let stand until set.

Yield: about 12 to 15 servings

GIFT-WRAPPED CHERRY PAN

You will need craft paper, cherry rubber stamp, red ink pad, green and red permanent fine-point markers, heavy-duty aluminum foil, 2 yds. of 1½"w ribbon, brown cardstock, and glue stick.

1. Cut a 24" x 36" rectangle from craft paper. Using rubber stamp and ink pad, stamp cherry design on paper; allow to dry. Referring to photo and using green marker, draw cherry stems.

2. Cover top of pan with heavy-duty aluminum foil. Wrap paper around pan as if wrapping a gift. Wrap ribbon around package and tie into a bow.

3. On scrap piece of craft paper, using rubber stamp and ink pad, stamp cherry design. Draw cherry stems using green marker. Cut out cherries and stems leaving ⅛" around edges.

4. Cut a 2½" x 3½" rectangle from cardstock to make gift tag. Using glue stick, adhere cherry and stem cutout to tag. Write greeting using red marker.

DELIGHTFULLY CREAMY DRESSING

Salad fans will clamor for a taste of this dressing that also doubles as a dip. A glass cylinder with ribbon and a circular tag make a classy container for the dressing, which can be lightened for your calorie-conscious friends and family by substituting low-fat sour cream.

CREAMY HONEY-HERB DRESSING

2	green onions, finely chopped
1	clove garlic, minced
1	container (8 ounces) sour cream
1½	tablespoons stone-ground mustard
1	tablespoon honey
1	tablespoon cider vinegar
1	teaspoon dried tarragon

Combine all ingredients in a food processor or blender until smooth.

Yield: about 1¼ cups dressing

COLORFUL BERRIES

These versatile red berries evoke the color and flavor of Christmas, especially when used in an assortment of cookies, scones, and muffins or as a topping for pound cake. Present them to a friend in an embellished glass jar complete with serving suggestions.

CANDIED CRANBERRIES

1 cup sugar
1 cup water
1½ cups fresh or frozen cranberries

Combine sugar and water in a medium saucepan. Cook over medium heat, stirring constantly until sugar dissolves. Using a pastry brush dipped in hot water, wash down any sugar crystals on sides of pan. Attach a candy thermometer to pan, making sure thermometer does not touch bottom of pan.

Bring mixture to a boil and cook, without stirring, until mixture reaches soft-ball stage or thermometer reaches approximately 235 degrees. Stir in cranberries and cook 2 to 3 minutes or until coated. Drain cranberries well, discarding syrup. Arrange cranberries in a single layer on wire rack. Cool completely. Store, covered, in refrigerator 4 to 6 weeks.

Yield: about 1½ cups cranberries

DECORATED MASON JAR

You will need mini colored beads, glass jar with screw-on lid, craft glue, glue stick, purchased gift tag, red permanent fine-point marker, 12" of ¼"w ribbon and 15" of 2"w sheer ribbon.

Allow glue to dry after each application.

1. Referring to photo and using craft glue, glue beads on jar in shapes as desired.
2. Place cranberries in jar and replace lid. Referring to photo, glue ribbon around edges of tag. Using marker, write recipe name and serving suggestions on tag.
3. Thread tag onto sheer ribbon. Tie ribbon around jar and into a bow.

SANTA'S SACK

Santa's sack can hold more than just presents—it can also be filled with Chunky Chocolate Cookies, ready to be delivered to good girls and boys.

CHUNKY CHOCOLATE COOKIES

1	cup butter, softened
1	cup sugar
1	cup firmly packed dark brown sugar
2	eggs
2	teaspoons vanilla extract
3	cups all-purpose flour
½	teaspoon baking soda
½	teaspoon salt
½	cup cocoa
1	package (11.5 ounces) semisweet chocolate chunks
1	cup coarsely chopped walnuts

Preheat oven to 350 degrees.

In a large bowl, beat butter and sugars at medium speed of an electric mixer until fluffy. Add eggs and vanilla; beat until smooth. In a medium bowl, combine flour, baking soda, salt, and cocoa. Add dry ingredients to creamed mixture; stir until a soft dough forms. Stir in chocolate and walnuts.

Drop by tablespoonfuls 2 inches apart onto a lightly greased baking sheet. Bake 10 minutes. Cool 1 minute on baking sheet; transfer cookies to a wire rack to cool completely. Store in an airtight container.

Yield: about 5 dozen cookies

NUTS OVER COOKIES

*R*oasted peanuts add a new texture to traditional peanut butter cookies.
Decorate a bright red bag with gingerbread men and fill it with cookies
to hang on a neighbor's door.

HONEY ROASTED PEANUT COOKIES

¾ cup butter, softened
¾ cup creamy peanut butter
1 cup firmly packed brown
    sugar
½ cup honey
2 eggs
1 teaspoon vanilla extract
2½ cup all-purpose flour
1 teaspoon baking soda
½ teaspoon salt
1¼ cups chopped honey
    roasted peanuts

In a large bowl, cream butter and peanut butter at medium speed of an electric mixer until fluffy; add brown sugar and honey, beating until smooth. Add eggs and vanilla; beat until smooth.

In a medium bowl, combine flour, baking soda, and salt; add to creamed mixture. Stir until a soft dough forms. Stir in peanuts. Cover and chill at least 2 hours. Preheat oven to 350 degrees.

Shape chilled dough into 1-inch balls; place balls 2 inches apart on lightly greased baking sheets. Flatten balls in a crisscross pattern with a fork dipped in flour. Bake 8 minutes or until edges are lightly browned. Cool 1 minute on baking sheets; cool completely on wire racks.
Yield: about 6½ dozen cookies

GINGERBREAD MAN GIFT BAG

You will need red paper gift bag, ruler, hole punch, 1 yd. ⅞"w plaid ribbon, brown paper, craft glue, six ½" dia. black buttons, and red tissue paper.

Allow glue to dry after each application.

1. Unfold and open gift bag. Using ruler, mark a line 2" down from top edge of bag on all sides. Referring to Fig. 1, page 141, cut away sides of bag, cutting to marked line. Triple-fold front and back sides to inside of bag with final folds along marked lines. Length of all sides of bag should measure 8½".

2. For ribbon handles, punch holes in bag front and back 1¼" in from side edges and ½" down from top edge. Cut ribbon in half. Thread ends of one ribbon length through holes in bag front. Tie ends of ribbon into knots to secure. Repeat to make handle for bag back.

3. Transfer gingerbread men pattern, page 141, to brown paper and cut out. Center and glue gingerbread men to front of bag, just below ribbon handles. Glue 2 buttons to front of each gingerbread man.

4. Place tissue paper in bag. Place cookies inside bag.

SCRUMPTIOUS SHORTBREAD

Serve a tray of chocolate pecan shortbread to someone and watch the recepient's mood brighten. This crafty tray, covered with colorful dots and lined with pretty wrapping paper, can be used later as a stylish home accent. The recipe makes enough for three gifts, so you can give two away and keep one for your family.

CHOCOLATE-PECAN SHORTBREAD

1 cup butter, softened
⅓ cup sugar
2 teaspoons vanilla extract
2 cups all-purpose flour
½ cup finely chopped pecans, toasted
3 squares (1 ounce each) semisweet chocolate, finely chopped
18 pecan halves
2 squares (1 ounce each) semisweet chocolate, melted

Preheat oven to 325 degrees.

In a large bowl, beat butter and sugar at medium speed of an electric mixer until fluffy. Add vanilla; beat until smooth. Add flour to creamed mixture; stir until a soft dough forms. Stir in pecans and finely chopped chocolate.

Divide dough into thirds. Roll one-third of dough into a 6-inch-diameter circle on an ungreased baking sheet. Flute edge of dough with handle of wooden spoon or fingertips. Score dough into 6 triangles. Repeat procedure twice with remaining two-thirds of dough. Bake 20 minutes or until edges are slightly golden. Remove from baking sheets; let cool on wire racks. Carefully separate into wedges.

Brush bottoms of pecan halves with melted chocolate; place 1 pecan half, chocolate-side down, in center of each wedge. Spoon remaining melted chocolate into a small plastic bag; snip a tiny hole in one corner. Pipe chocolate over pecan halves.

Yield: about 18 shortbread wedges

POLKA DOT TRAY

You will need wooden tray, white and green paints, paintbrush, decorative paper, craft glue, green cardstock, hole punch, and 8" of 1½"w ribbon.

Allow paint to dry after each application.

1. Paint tray white. Once paint dries, paint small dots on tray using green paint and end of paintbrush.
2. Cut decorative paper to fit inside tray. Using glue, adhere paper inside tray.
3. Cut 2½" circle from cardstock. Using end of paintbrush and white paint, paint small dots on cardstock circle. Referring to photo, punch hole in tag and thread onto ribbon. Tie ribbon to tray handle.

Chocolate Pecan Shortbead

47

A JEWEL OF A COOKIE

*A*dd a splash of color to Christmas by baking a batch of these bright cookies for a friend. Get your creative juices flowing and use a variety of preserves to fill the plate of cookies. Place in a gift box that's large enough to hold the cookies without having to stack them.

JEWELED THUMBPRINTS

1	cup butter, softened
½	cup firmly packed light brown sugar
1	egg, separated
1	teaspoon vanilla extract
½	teaspoon almond extract
1	cup all-purpose flour
2	cups regular oats, toasted
2	teaspoons water
1¼	cups finely chopped pecans, almonds, or walnuts
½	cup fruit preserves

In a large bowl, beat butter and sugar at medium speed of an electric mixer until fluffy. Add egg yolk and extracts; beat until smooth. Add flour and oats to creamed mixture; stir until a soft dough forms. Cover and chill dough 30 minutes.

Preheat oven to 300 degrees.

Shape chilled dough into 1-inch balls. Beat egg white and water at medium speed of an electric mixer 1 minute or until frothy. Dip balls in egg white mixture and roll in nuts. Place 2 inches apart on greased baking sheets. Press thumb in center of each ball to make an indentation. Bake 15 minutes. Spoon about ½ teaspoon preserves into each indentation. Bake 15 minutes. Transfer cookies to wire racks and cool completely. *Yield:* about 3 dozen cookies

SPEEDY SUPPER

This ready made pot pie with its fluffy biscuit topping just needs to be popped into the oven for reheating. It's a great gift as well as nice for you to have on hand for those surprise visits from holiday well-wishers. Use a disposable pan for easy clean up and attach a decorative tag complete with reheating instructions.

QUICK CHICKEN POT PIE

3	cups chopped cooked chicken or turkey
2	cans (10¾ ounces each) cream of chicken soup
1	cup chicken broth
1	can (15 ounces) mixed vegetables, drained and rinsed
½	teaspoon poultry seasoning
2	cups biscuit mix
1	carton (8 ounces) sour cream
1	cup milk

Preheat oven to 375 degrees.

In a large bowl, combine chicken, soup, broth, mixed vegetables, and poultry seasoning. Pour chicken mixture into a lightly greased 9 x 13-inch baking dish.

In a medium bowl, combine biscuit mix, sour cream, and milk; pour over chicken mixture.

Bake 50 to 60 minutes or until top is golden brown, covering edges with aluminum foil after 50 minutes to prevent overbrowning. Let stand 5 minutes before serving.
Yield: about 6 servings pot pie

To Make Ahead: Use a 9 x 13-inch disposable aluminum pan. Cover and freeze after pouring biscuit mixture over chicken mixture. Place in a preheated 375-degree oven and bake 1 hour and 10 minutes.

If using disposable aluminum pan, it's best to remove it from the oven by slipping a sturdy baking sheet underneath pan for additional stability.

ORNAMENT TAG

You will need two 3½" dia. decorative wooden circles, paintbrush, red and gold paints, handmade paper, black permanent fine-point marker, glue stick, drill, 18" of 1½"w sheer ribbon, 25" of 2½"w woven ribbon, and a sprig of greenery.

Allow paint to dry after each application.

1. Paint front and back of wooden circles using red paint.
2. Referring to photo, brush over front and back of wooden circles using gold paint.
3. Tear a 3" dia. circle from handmade paper. Using marker, write greeting on paper circle.
4. Using glue stick, adhere paper circle to one side of one wooden circle.
5. Drill small hole in top of each wooden circle. Thread wooden circles onto sheer ribbon and tie into a knot.
6. Tie woven ribbon around dish and lid and into a knot. Referring to photo, tie sheer ribbon with wooden ornaments onto woven ribbon. Insert sprig of greenery, if desired.

BROWNIES AT THEIR BEST

These fudgy brownies look like they were purchased at a fancy bakery, but you simply make the design with a toothpick. The unique packaging ensures that the brownies will not get ruined during transport.

MOCHA FUDGE WALNUT BROWNIES

5   squares (1 ounce each) unsweetened chocolate
½   cup butter
3   eggs
2   tablespoons light corn syrup
1   tablespoon vanilla extract
1¼   cups sugar
¾   cup plus 2 tablespoons all-purpose flour
⅛   teaspoon salt
½   cup chopped walnuts
1   tablespoon instant coffee granules
Mocha Fudge Glaze
1   square (1 ounce) white chocolate, melted

Preheat oven to 325 degrees. Line a 9-inch square baking pan with aluminum foil extending foil over ends of pan; grease foil.

In a small saucepan over low heat, melt unsweetened chocolate and butter. Transfer melted chocolate mixture to a small bowl; cool completely. Add eggs, 1 at a time, to cooled chocolate, beating until well blended. Stir in corn syrup and vanilla.

In a medium bowl, combine sugar, flour, salt, walnuts, and coffee granules. Stir flour mixture into chocolate mixture. Spread batter into prepared pan. Bake 25 minutes (brownies will not test done.) Cool in pan on a wire rack.

Spread Mocha Fudge Glaze over brownies. Place melted white chocolate in a small heavy-duty resealable plastic bag; snip off 1 corner of bag to create a small opening. Drizzle chocolate in parallel lines, ½ inch apart, across brownies. Pull point of a toothpick through white chocolate lines to create perpendicular pattern. Chill, covered, 15 minutes or until glaze is set. Use ends of foil to lift brownies from pan. Cut into 2-inch squares.
Yield: about 20 brownies

Mocha Fudge Glaze
⅓   cup whipping cream
1   teaspoon instant coffee granules
3   squares (1 ounce each) semisweet chocolate, coarsely chopped

In a small saucepan, combine whipping cream and coffee granules. Bring to a boil over medium heat. Remove from heat; stir until coffee dissolves. Place chocolate in a medium bowl; pour hot coffee mixture over chocolate. Let stand 5 minutes; stir until smooth. Let stand 15 minutes or until slightly thickened.
Yield: about ½ cup glaze

FANCY CARDBOARD COVER

You will need a square piece of cardboard, resealable freezer bag, tissue paper, corrugated cardboard, and a ribbon bow.

1. Place brownies on a square piece of sturdy cardboard, cut a few inches shorter and narrower than resealable freezer bag.
2. Place brownies inside bag and seal, trapping some air.
3. Referring to photo, wrap bag with tissue paper, corrugated cardboard, and bow.

51

JAZZED UP RICE

A busy family would be overjoyed to receive this pre-packaged rice mix chock-full of apricots and pistachios. The rice makes a spiffy side when paired with chicken or fish. A miniature wooden sleigh holds enough mix for four people.

JASMINE RICE PILAF MIX

2   teaspoons chicken bouillon
      granules
¼   cup chopped dried
      apricots
1   cup uncooked jasmine rice
¼   cup chopped pistachios
1   teaspoon dried parsley
¼   teaspoon salt

Combine all ingredients. Store in an airtight container. Give the gift with instructions for preparing rice.
Yield: about 1½ cups rice mix

To prepare rice: Combine rice mix, 1 tablespoon butter, and 2 cups water in a saucepan; bring to a boil. Reduce heat to low. Cover and cook 20 minutes. Let stand 5 minutes. Fluff with a fork.
Yield: about 4 servings rice

BASKET OF COLORS

Reward a busy mom with a gift basket of colored sugars and a recipe for Brown Sugar Cookies, a delightful twist on the traditional variety. Small, glass clamp-top jars provide an inexpensive and fun way to deliver the sugars. Use any leftover sugars to decorate cakes, cupcakes, or other desserts.

BROWN SUGAR COOKIES

1	cup butter, softened
1½	cups firmly packed dark brown sugar
1	egg
1	teaspoon vanilla extract
3	cups all-purpose flour
1	teaspoon baking soda
½	teaspoon salt

Colored sugars

Preheat oven to 350 degrees.

Beat butter at medium speed of an electric mixer until fluffy. Gradually add brown sugar, beating well. Add egg and vanilla, beating well.

In a large bowl, combine flour, soda, and salt; add to creamed mixture, beating just until blended.

Roll dough to ¼-inch thickness between two sheets of waxed paper. Cut with 3½-inch cookie cutters. Place 1 inch apart on ungreased baking sheets. Sprinkle cookies with colored sugars.

Bake 10 to 12 minutes. Let cookies cool 1 minute on baking sheets, and transfer to wire racks to cool completely.

Yield: about 1½ dozen cookies

Colored Sugars

1½ cups sugar
Red, green, and yellow paste food coloring

Place ½ cup sugar and a small amount of food coloring in a jar or resealable plastic bag. Stir until color is evenly mixed with sugar. Repeat with remaining sugar and other colors.

Note: For more intense colors we used food color paste, found in the cake decorating section of crafts stores.

CHRISTMAS CRUNCH

Bite into this brittle for a big burst of cinnamon. We've loaded pecans in crunchy candy for an old-fashioned favorite. Purchase an embellished box and line it with a dish towel for a charming container.

PECAN-CINNAMON BRITTLE

1½	cups finely chopped pecans
2	tablespoons butter, cut into pieces
1	teaspoon baking soda
¾	teaspoon ground cinnamon
1	cup sugar
½	cup light corn syrup
⅓	cup water
⅛	teaspoon salt

In a small bowl, combine pecans, butter, baking soda, and cinnamon, and set aside.

In a large saucepan, combine sugar, corn syrup, water, and salt. Stirring constantly, cook over medium-low heat until sugar dissolves. Cover and cook 2 to 3 minutes to wash down any sugar crystals on sides of pan. Attach a candy thermometer to pan, making sure thermometer does not touch bottom of pan. Increase heat to medium and bring to a boil. Cook, without stirring, until mixture reaches hard-crack stage (approximately 300 to 310 degrees). Test about ½ teaspoon mixture in ice water. Mixture will form brittle threads in ice water

and remain brittle when removed from water. Remove from heat. Stir in reserved pecan mixture until butter melts. Pour mixture onto a greased baking sheet. Use 2 wooden spoons to pull warm candy until stretched thin. Cool completely. Break into pieces. Store in an airtight container.
Yield: about 1 pound candy

54

RENDEZVOUS WITH REINDEER

Y*ou won't find cookies this cute and this easy anywhere else. Starting with refrigerated dough makes this recipe fun and simple. To present, wrap each cookie in cellophane and tie with holiday ribbon.*

EASY REINDEER COOKIES

1   package (20 ounces) refrigerated sliceable peanut butter cookie dough
60 mini pretzel twists (2 inches each)
60 semisweet chocolate morsels
30 red candy-coated chocolate pieces

Freeze dough 15 minutes.

Cut dough into 30 (¼-inch-thick) slices. Place 4 inches apart on ungreased baking sheets. Using thumb and fore-finger, pinch in each slice about two-thirds of the way down to shape face.

Press a pretzel on each side of larger end for antlers.

Press in chocolate morsels for eyes.

Bake at 350 degrees 9 to 11 minutes or until lightly browned.

Remove from oven, and press in red candy for nose. Let stand 2 minutes; remove to wire racks to cool.

Yield: about 2½ dozen cookies

DELIGHTFUL DIP

*T*his *creamy holiday treat will become a favorite for children of all ages with its sweet and tangy flavor, and you'll love how easy it is to whip up. Serve it in a glass bowl decorated with beaded trim and include gingerbread cookies or apples for dipping.*

SWEET ORANGE DIP

1   can (14 ounces) sweetened
      condensed milk
1   can (6 ounces) frozen orange
      juice concentrate, thawed
      and undiluted
3   tablespoons orange zest

Combine all ingredients in a small bowl, stirring until blended; chill. Serve with gingerbread cookies or apple slices.
Yield: about 2 cups dip

TRIMMED JAR AND NAPKIN

You will need craft glue, 18" of beaded trim, 4½" dia. glass bowl, 6" square linen napkin, 14" of ⅛"w orange sheer ribbon, and yellow and orange paint pens.

1. Using craft glue, adhere trim to edge of glass bowl.
2. Referring to photo, weave ribbon through hemstitching around edges of napkin. Glue ribbon ends onto underside of napkin. Using paint pens, make dots around edges of napkin.

TOPSY-TURVY APRICOT CAKE

The convenience of a cake mix is a plus in this apricot-and-almond-studded cake that tastes as scrumptious as it looks. A stenciled charger holds the cake in all its glory—ready to give to a deserving friend.

APRICOT-ALMOND UPSIDE-DOWN CAKE

- ¼ cup butter, melted
- 1 can (15¼ ounces) apricot halves, drained
- ⅓ cup firmly packed light brown sugar
- ⅓ cup slivered almonds, toasted
- 1 package (16 ounces) pound cake mix (we used Betty Crocker)
- 1 teaspoon vanilla extract
- 1 teaspoon almond extract

Preheat oven to 350 degrees.

Grease sides of a 9-inch round cakepan; pour butter into cake pan. Arrange apricot halves, cut side up, in pan. Sprinkle with brown sugar and almonds.

Prepare pound cake mix according to package directions; stir in extracts. Pour batter over apricots and almonds.

Bake 50 to 60 minutes or until toothpick inserted in center of cake comes out clean. Run a knife around edges of cake to loosen; invert onto a serving plate.

Yield: one 9-inch cake

EMBELLISHED CHARGER

You will need 13" dia. food-safe charger, gold paint pen, green paper, cream paper, glue stick, and gold permanent fine-point marker.

1. Referring to photo, draw design around edge of charger using paint pen.

2. Cut a 3½" x 6" rectangle from green paper. Fold in half to make gift tag. Cut a 3½" x 2" rectangle from cream paper. Center and adhere cream rectangle to tag using glue stick.

3. Using marker, write recipe name on cream rectangle.

LEMON-GINGER DELIGHT

*T*he gift of dessert is always well received, and our Drenched Gingerbread
Pudding is no exception. Infused with a lemon syrup and dressed with
golden lemon curls, it's a feast for the eyes, as well as the palette.
Present it in a basket laced with ribbon and paired with
gingerbread cookie cutters.

DRENCHED GINGERBREAD PUDDING

½ cup butter, softened
¼ cup firmly packed brown
 sugar
1 egg
⅔ cup molasses
2⅓ cups all-purpose flour
1½ teaspoons baking soda
½ teaspoon salt
1½ teaspoons ground ginger
¾ teaspoon ground cinnamon
¼ teaspoon ground cloves
1 cup hot water
1 cup sifted confectioners
 sugar
½ teaspoon grated lemon zest
¼ cup fresh lemon juice
Garnish: Lemon curls

Preheat oven to 350 degrees.
In a large bowl, beat butter at
medium-high speed of an electric
mixer until creamy; gradually add
brown sugar, beating well. Add
egg and molasses, beating well.
Combine flour, baking soda, salt,
ginger, cinnamon, and cloves; add
to creamed mixture alternately
with hot water, beginning and
ending with flour mixture. Mix
after each addition. Pour batter
into a greased and floured 8-inch
disposable aluminum square pan.
Bake 30 minutes or until a
toothpick inserted in center of
pudding comes out clean.
 Combine confectioners sugar,
lemon zest, and lemon juice in a
small saucepan; stir well. Bring
mixture to a boil; boil 1 minute
and remove from heat. Using a
toothpick, poke holes in top of
pudding. Slowly pour syrup
mixture over pudding. Cool
completely on a wire rack. Garnish
with lemon curls, if desired.
Yield: about 9 servings pudding

COOKIE CUTTER BASKET

You will need a 10" square basket,
2 yds. of decorative wired-edge
ribbon, gingerbread man cookie
cutters in graduated sizes, hole
punch, red permanent fine-point
marker, decorative-edge craft
scissors, and red tissue paper.

1. Referring to photo and
beginning and ending at one side
of basket, lace ribbon through
openings in basket to cover rim.
Tie ribbon ends where they meet
into bow.
2. Stack cookie cutters inside each
other. Referring to photo, tuck
underneath bow on basket.
3. Using craft scissors, trim edges
of tissue paper. Line basket with
tissue paper before placing
pudding inside basket.

SPICE UP THE HOLIDAYS

*H*elp *a friend add some heat to a cold winter night with a gift from the Southwest. The dry mix can be used to season poultry and rice or to make the marinade for fajitas. Attach colored ribbon to spruce up the simple packaging.*

SOUTHWESTERN SEASONING BLEND

¼	cup dried parsley flakes
¼	cup dried oregano
2	tablespoons dried thyme
2	tablespoons cumin seeds
1	tablespoon black peppercorns
1	teaspoon paprika
3	dried red chile pepper pods

Place all ingredients in a food processor or coffee grinder; process until spices are blended and peppercorns are a medium grind.
Yield: about ½ cup mix

FAJITA MARINADE

¼	cup vegetable oil
2	tablespoons lime juice
1	tablespoon Southwestern Seasoning Blend
1	teaspoon minced garlic
¼	teaspoon salt

In a small bowl, combine all ingredients and stir with a wire whisk until thoroughly mixed.

Note: The marinade can easily be doubled or tripled to fit any size container.

SPREAD IT ON THICK

*S*atisfy the peanut butter lover on your list by delivering a jar of this nutty spread, nestled into a basket with plenty of graham crackers and apples for spreading the blend.

PEANUT BUTTER SPREAD

1	package (8 ounces) cream cheese, softened
1½	cups creamy peanut butter
½	cup sifted confectioners sugar
1	tablespoon milk
⅓	cup chopped dry roasted peanuts

Combine cream cheese, peanut butter, confectioners sugar, and milk in a small bowl; beat at medium speed with an electric mixer 1 minute or until smooth. Top spread with peanuts and serve with apple wedges or graham crackers. Store in an airtight container in refrigerator.
Yield: about 2 cups spread

HANDLED TRAY

You will need a small tin tray with handles, wired artificial red berries and leaves, raffia ribbon, brown cardstock, red permanent fine-point marker, hole punch, jar with lid, cellophane, and 18" of ¼"w ribbon.

1. Referring to photo, attach small bunches of berries to tray handles by wrapping wired part of berries around the handles. Repeat to attach 1 or 2 leaves to each handle.
2. Cut a long length of raffia. Knot one end of raffia around one side of one tray handle. Wrap raffia tightly around entire handle concealing wire ends of berries and leaves. Knot raffia at opposite end of handle. Repeat for opposite tray handle.
3. Cut a 2" x 4" rectangle from cardstock and fold in half lengthwise to make gift tag. Using red marker, write recipe name on tag. Using hole punch, cut 2 holes about ½" apart near fold in tag.
4. Cut a length of raffia and thread it through both holes in tag. Referring to photo, tuck 1 or 2 berries into holes in tag. Pour spread into jar, and tie tag around neck of jar.
5. Wrap stacks of graham crackers in cellophane. Cut a 9" length of ribbon and tie around cellophane and into a bow on top of stack.

ASIAN-INSPIRED SNACK

Our flavorful Chinese chips will prove to be a requested snack at any holiday gathering with their salty-sweet taste and golden hue.

CRISPY CHINESE CHIPS

17	fresh or frozen wonton wrappers, thawed
1	tablespoon soy sauce
½	teaspoon sugar
½	teaspoon peeled, minced gingerroot
1	teaspoon dark sesame oil
½	teaspoon garlic salt

Dash of hot sauce
Sesame seeds

Preheat oven to 375 degrees.
Cut wonton wrappers in half diagonally; set aside. Combine soy sauce, sugar, gingerroot, sesame oil, garlic salt, and hot sauce in a small bowl. Place wonton wrappers in a single layer on a greased baking sheet; brush tops lightly with soy sauce mixture. Sprinkle evenly with sesame seeds. Bake 7 minutes or until wonton wrappers are lightly browned and crisp; let cool completely. Store in an airtight container.
Yield: about 34 chips

HOLLY STENCIL BAG

You will need tracing paper, white cardstock, craft knife, hole punch, silver acrylic paint, stencil brush, green paper bag, green and black permanent fine-point markers, spiral paper clips, and 36" of ¼"w ribbon.

Allow paint to dry after each application.

1. Trace holly patterns, page 142, onto tracing paper; cut out. Cut a 1½" x 3½" rectangle from cardstock. To make stencil, transfer holly patterns to cardstock and cut out using craft knife.
2. Referring to photo and using hole punch, punch 3 holes to create berries in cardstock stencil.
3. Use silver paint and stencil brush to paint holly and berries on bag.
4. Cut a 2" x 3" rectangle from cardstock to make gift tag. Referring to photo, draw border around tag using green marker. Write recipe name using black marker.
5. Place clips along top of bag to close. Slide tag under several clips.
6. Cut three 12" lengths of ribbon. Tie lengths onto end and middle clips, knotting ends.

CHERRY CRAVINGS

Deliver Christmas tidings to friends in cherry-topped tins filled with Pistachio-Cherry Fudge Rolls.

PISTACHIO-CHERRY FUDGE ROLLS

1½	pounds white baking chocolate, chopped
1	can (14 ounces) sweetened condensed milk
1	cup finely chopped pistachios
1	cup chopped red and green candied cherries
1	teaspoon vanilla extract
⅛	teaspoon salt
1½	cups finely chopped pistachios

Line an 8-inch square baking pan with waxed paper, extending paper over ends of pan.

In top of a double boiler, combine chocolate and milk over boiling water. Reduce heat to low. Stirring constantly, cook mixture until chocolate melts and mixture is smooth. Stir in 1 cup pistachios, cherries, vanilla, and salt. Spread fudge into prepared pan; chill 2 hours or until almost firm.

Use ends of waxed paper to lift fudge from pan; remove paper. Cut fudge into four 2 x 8-inch strips. Shape each section into a 10-inch-long log. Roll logs in remaining pistachios, pressing nuts firmly into fudge. Chill 2 additional hours or until firm. Cut each log into ½-inch slices. Store in an airtight container in refrigerator.
Yield: about 80 fudge rolls

CHERRY CONTAINER

You will need red and white canister with lid, hot glue gun, artificial cherries, and 1½ yds. of 1½"w ribbon.

1. Referring to photo and using hot glue gun, adhere cherries to center of lid.
2. Cut a 16" length of ribbon. Using hot glue gun, adhere one end of ribbon inside canister.

Referring to photo, wrap ribbon around canister, across bottom, up opposite side, and adhere remaining end of ribbon inside canister.
3. Cut a 25" length of ribbon. Referring to photo, wrap one ribbon length around canister and into a bow. Trim tails of bow.
4. Layer candies in container with waxed paper between layers.

SAVORY SPREAD

*S*pread some holiday cheer with a jar of creamy, flavor-packed Roasted Garlic-Parmesan Spread. To package it, personalize a gift box with your favorite holiday sayings or song verses and attach an attractive spreader for a thoughtful touch.

ROASTED GARLIC-PARMESAN SPREAD

2   large heads garlic, unpeeled
2   tablespoons olive oil
2   packages (8 ounces each) cream cheese, softened
1   cup butter, softened
1   cup freshly grated Parmesan cheese
1   tablespoon dried Italian seasoning
½   teaspoon freshly ground pepper
1   jar (4 ounces) diced pimento, drained

Preheat oven to 350 degrees.
Place garlic on aluminum foil; drizzle with oil, and wrap. Bake 45 minutes to 1 hour. Cool. Cut off pointed ends of garlic; squeeze pulp from cloves. Beat cream cheese and butter at medium speed of an electric mixer until creamy. Add pulp, Parmesan cheese, seasoning, pepper, and pimento; beat well. Spread on baguette slices or crackers. Refrigerate up to 2 weeks.
Yield: about 4 cups spread

CHRISTMAS TURNOVERS

A flaky crust envelopes the flavorful filling that's loaded with cranberries and mincemeat—a tradition at Christmas. Pack these turnovers into little paper bags for easy transport and pass them out to awaiting hands. They're wonderful with a cup of coffee for breakfast or as a late-night dessert.

CRAN-CHERRY MINCEMEAT TURNOVERS

- 1 package (9 ounces) condensed mincemeat (we used None-Such)
- 1 can (16 ounces) whole-berry cranberry sauce
- 1 cup cranberry-apple juice
- 1 can (21 ounces) cherry pie filling
- ½ cup chopped pecans, toasted
- 2 teaspoons grated orange zest (optional)
- 2 packages (15 ounces each) refrigerated piecrusts

Confectioners sugar

Preheat oven to 425 degrees. In a large saucepan, combine mincemeat, cranberry sauce, and juice. Cook over medium-high heat until mixture boils. Stirring constantly, cook over medium-high heat 6 to 7 minutes or until thickened. Cool completely. Stir in pie filling, pecans, and orange zest.

Unfold 1 pie crust and roll into a 13-inch-diameter circle. Cut circle into five 5-inch circles, re-rolling scraps if necessary. Moisten edges of circles, and spoon about ¼ cup filling into center of each. Pinch edges to seal. Place on greased baking sheets. Crimp edges with a fork. Repeat procedure with remaining pie crusts and filling.

Bake 10 to 12 minutes or until crusts are golden brown. Cool completely. Sprinkle with confectioners sugar.

Yield: about 21 turnovers

Note: To prevent filling from leaking while sealing, do not fold dough over filling on work surface. Instead, gather sides of dough together over filling; pick up and place in palm of 1 hand. Use fingers of both hands to seal dough.

PRESENTS IN A PLANTER

A Sunday brunch wouldn't be complete without fresh coffee and these tasty muffins packed with the flavor of bacon and cheese in every bite. Easy to make and easy to eat, these muffins are the perfect breakfast treat! A decoupaged plastic planter completes this quick gift.

BACON-AND-CHEESE MUFFINS

- 1¾ cups all-purpose flour
- 2½ teaspoons baking powder
- ½ teaspoon salt
- 2 tablespoons sugar
- 10 slices bacon, cooked and crumbled
- ½ cup (2 ounces) shredded sharp Cheddar cheese
- 1 large egg, lightly beaten
- ¾ cup milk
- ⅓ cup vegetable oil

Preheat oven to 400 degrees.

Line a muffin pan with paper muffin cups, or grease and flour muffin pan.

In a large bowl, combine flour, baking powder, salt, sugar, bacon, and cheese; make a well in center of mixture. In a small bowl, combine egg, milk, and oil. Add to dry ingredients; stir just until moistened.

Fill muffin cups about two-thirds full. Bake 20 minutes or until golden. Remove from pans immediately.

Yield: about 1 dozen muffins

DECOUPAGED PLANTER

You will need rectangular plastic planter, Christmas wrapping paper, sponge paintbrush, decoupage glue, 3 yds. of 1½"w ribbon, 3 yds. of 1⅜"w ribbon, and 2 cloth napkins.

Allow glue to dry after each application.

1. Wash and dry planter.
2. Tear wrapping paper into approximately 2" to 3" pieces. Working on a small area at a time and using sponge paintbrush, apply decoupage glue to sides and rim of planter. Place piece of torn paper in glue on planter. Brush glue on top of paper piece. Continue gluing and overlapping paper pieces to cover planter.
3. Holding both ribbons as one and referring to photo, tie ribbons into a bow around planter. Line planter with napkins. Place muffins in planter.

Note: Once muffins are gone, napkins can be removed and planter can be used to force amaryllis or paperwhite bulbs.

*T*he star of any breakfast is a stack of fluffy pancakes hot off the griddle, waiting to be drenched in butter and syrup. Add cornmeal to the mix and you have a heartier texture and fuller flavor. A great idea for busy holiday mornings, simply wrap the dry mix and attach a tag with recipe for making the pancakes.

HEARTY CORNMEAL PANCAKE MIX

1	cup all-purpose flour
3	tablespoons yellow cornmeal
2	tablespoons brown sugar
1	tablespoon baking powder
½	teaspoon baking soda
½	teaspoon salt

Combine all ingredients in a medium bowl, stirring until blended. Spoon mix into a heavy-duty, resealable plastic bag; remove air, and seal.

To make pancakes: Add 1 egg, 1 cup buttermilk, and 1 tablespoon vegetable oil to pancake mix. Stir, using a wire whisk until blended. Yield: about 1½ cups mix

STAR-WRAPPED BAG

You will need resealable plastic bag, cellophane bag, tissue paper, 1 yd. of 2½"w wired ribbon, tracing paper, cream paper, gold paint pen, brown permanent fine-point marker, and hole punch.

1. Place mix in plastic bag. Wrap tissue paper around plastic bag and insert into cellophane bag.
2. Tie ribbon into a bow around cellophane bag. Trim ribbon ends.
3. Trace star pattern, page 143, onto tracing paper; cut out.

Transfer star pattern to cream paper; cut out. Using gold paint pen, draw border around star and make dots on each point of star. Write recipe name and instructions using marker. Punch hole in star, and thread onto ribbon.

THREE CHEERS FOR CHEESE

*P*resent this three-cheese egg casserole studded with crispy bacon to a breakfast lover for an extra special holiday brunch. Since it has to chill for eight hours, make it the night before you plan to give it. Disposable baking pans make practical packaging, and a little adornment on top creates a snazzy presentation.

TRIPLE-CHEESE OMELET CASSEROLE

12	bacon slices
½	cup chopped onion
¼	cup chopped green pepper
1	package (26 ounces) frozen shredded hash browns, thawed
2	cups (8 ounces) shredded Swiss cheese
2	packages (3 ounces each) cream cheese, softened
6	eggs
½	cup milk
½	cup freshly grated Parmesan cheese
½	teaspoon salt
½	teaspoon pepper

Cook bacon in a large skillet until crisp; remove bacon, reserving 2 tablespoons drippings in skillet. Crumble bacon, and set aside.

Cook onion and green pepper in drippings over medium-high heat, stirring constantly, until tender.

Place hash browns in a greased disposable 3-quart baking pan; sprinkle evenly with Swiss cheese and half of bacon. Top evenly with vegetable mixture.

Beat cream cheese at medium speed of an electric mixer until creamy. Add eggs and milk; beat until smooth. Add Parmesan cheese, salt, and pepper; beat just until blended. Pour cream cheese mixture over vegetable mixture; sprinkle with remaining half of bacon. Cover and chill 8 to 12 hours.

Uncover and bake at 350 degrees 35 to 40 minutes or until set and lightly browned.
Yield: about 8 servings casserole

Note: We used the Reyonlds' PotLux 12½ x 9-inch disposable baking pan. It needs to be placed on a sturdy baking sheet when baked.

COOKIES FOR TEACHER

*I*nstead of an apple for Christmas, present a teacher with a clever blackboard-inspired bag filled with Spiced Apple-Oatmeal Cookies. Seal the bag with a piece of chalk and be sure to spell the teacher's name correctly!

SPICED APPLE-OATMEAL COOKIES

¼	cup butter, softened
½	cup shortening
1¼	cups firmly packed dark brown sugar
¾	cup sugar
2	eggs
1¼	cups cinnamon applesauce
1½	teaspoons vanilla extract
3	cups all-purpose flour
1	teaspoon baking soda
½	teaspoon salt
2	teaspoons ground cinnamon
½	teaspoon ground nutmeg
¼	teaspoon ground cloves
3	cups quick-cooking oats, uncooked
1	cup chopped dried apple
1	cup raisins

Preheat oven to 350 degrees.

In a large bowl, cream butter, shortening, and sugars at medium speed of an electric mixer until fluffy. Add eggs, applesauce, and vanilla; beat until smooth.

Combine flour, soda, salt, cinnamon, nutmeg, and cloves; add to creamed mixture; stir until a soft dough forms. Stir in oats, apple, and raisins. Drop by tablespoonfuls 2 inches apart onto ungreased baking sheets. Bake 12

minutes. Cool 1 minute on baking sheets; cool completely on wire racks.

Yield: about 4½ dozen cookies

BLACKBOARD GIFT BAG

You will need white dimensional paint, black paper bag, red acrylic paint, white chalk, 24" of ⅝"w ribbon, and hot glue gun.

Allow paint and glue to dry after each application.

1. Referring to photo, use white dimensional paint to write message on lower front of gift bag. Referring to photo and using red paint, paint peppermint swirls on chalk.

2. Place cookies inside bag. Fold top 2½" of bag to front. Cut two holes approximately ⅜" in diameter and ¾" apart in folded area of bag. Insert painted chalk through holes.

3. Tie ribbon into bow and glue to center top of bag using hot glue gun.

POPCORN PRESENTS

These popcorn balls are individually wrapped presents, ready to be handed out to your favorite elves. Use clear plastic wrap and a variety of colored pipe cleaners to package these yummy treats.

OLD-FASHIONED POPCORN BALLS

2	cups firmly packed dark brown sugar
¾	cup light corn syrup
¾	cup water
½	teaspoon salt
½	cup butter
1	teaspoon vanilla extract
6	quarts popped popcorn
1	cup pistachios, coarsely chopped

Butter sides of a heavy medium saucepan. Combine sugar, syrup, water, and salt in saucepan. Stirring gently, cook over medium-low heat until sugar dissolves. Using a pastry brush dipped in hot water, wash down any sugar crystals on sides of pan. Attach a candy thermometer to pan, making sure thermometer does not touch bottom of pan. Increase heat to medium, and bring to a boil. Cook, without stirring, until mixture reaches hard-ball stage (approximately 254 degrees). Remove from heat and stir in butter and vanilla.

Place popcorn and pistachios in a large pan. Pour hot syrup over top, stirring well with a wooden spoon. Grease hands with butter, and shape mixture into balls. Place on waxed paper to dry.

Yield: about 2 dozen popcorn balls

CHENILLE PIPE CLEANER WRAP

You will need clear plastic wrap, red and green chenille pipe cleaners, white cardstock, decorative-edge craft scissors, black permanent fine-point marker, craft knife, and 10" of ¼"w ribbon.

1. Wrap popcorn ball in plastic wrap.
2. Lay two pipe cleaners in shape of a plus mark on a table. Place wrapped popcorn ball in center. Wrap ends of pipe cleaners up around ball. Referring to photo, form two ends of pipe cleaners into loops and two ends into trails.
3. Cut a 2" x 3½" rectangle from cardstock using craft scissors to make gift tag. Write recipe name on tag using marker. Cut slit in tag using craft knife. Thread tag onto ribbon.

HEAVEN SENT

*F*riends who savor the aroma of freshly baked bread will think our Parmesan Flatbread is
heavenly. Cut bread into slices to tuck into the paper bags and adorn with wooden
angel ornaments for keepsake Christmas tree decorations.

PARMESAN FLATBREAD

1   package dry yeast
1   tablespoon sugar
1¼ cups warm water (100 to
    110 degrees)
5   cups bread flour, divided
2   tablespoons grated
    Parmesan cheese
2   teaspoons salt
¾   cup beer, at room
    temperature
2   tablespoons olive oil
3   tablespoons yellow
    cornmeal
Olive oil
½   cup freshly grated Parmesan
    cheese
2   teaspoons coarse salt

Dissolve yeast and sugar in
warm water; let stand 5 minutes.
In a large bowl, combine 1 cup
flour, cheese, and salt. Add yeast
mixture, beer, and 2 tablespoons
olive oil; stir well. Cover and let
stand in a warm place (85 degrees),
free from drafts, 30 minutes or
until dough is very bubbly.

Gradually stir in enough of the
remaining flour to make a soft
dough. Turn dough out onto a
heavily floured surface and knead
until smooth and elastic (about 8
minutes). Let dough rest 10
minutes. Sprinkle two 14-inch
pizza pans evenly with cornmeal;

set aside. Divide dough into 2
equal portions. Roll 1 portion of
dough into a 14-inch circle and
place on prepared pizza pan;
press to edges. Repeat procedure
with remaining dough. Prick
dough several times with a fork.
Brush each circle generously with
olive oil and sprinkle evenly with
freshly grated Parmesan cheese
and coarse salt. Cover and let rise
in a warm place, free from drafts,
20 minutes. Bake at 425 degrees
15 minutes or until golden. Serve
warm.
Yield: 2 flatbreads

PAPER POUCHES WITH ANGEL ORNAMENT

You will need an unfinished
wooden angel ornament, white
acrylic paint, silver and gold glitter
dimensional paints, raffia ribbon,
brown craft paper, craft glue,
brown cardstock, silver paint pen,
and hole punch.

*Allow paint to dry after each
application.*

1. Paint angel ornament using
white paint. Referring to photo,
outline angel halo, hands, and feet
using gold dimensional paint. Paint
angel gown using silver dimensional
paint. Cut a length of raffia for
ornament hanger. Thread raffia
through hole in ornament and tie
into a knot.
2. Cut a 15" x 15" square from
brown craft paper. Fold bottom
corners toward center of square.
Fold each side toward center
overlapping 1". Glue overlapping
side edges in place. Fold
remaining bottom edge toward
center. Glue bottom in place to
make bag.
3. Cut a 2" x 4" rectangle from
cardstock and fold in half
lengthwise to make gift tag. Using
silver paint pen, write recipe name
on gift tag.
4. Using hole punch, punch hole
in corner of tag through fold.
Punch hole in each side of bag
through both layers 3" below bag
opening.
5. Cut a length of raffia ribbon.
Referring to photo, thread raffia
from back of bag through each
side hole. Thread tag onto one end
of raffia and thread angel
ornament hanger onto opposite
end of raffia. Tie raffia into bow so
that ornament hangs in center of
bag.

CAP OFF AN EVENING

*C*elebrate the holidays by bringing a bottle of Praline Liqueur as a gift to a neighbor's Christmas party. Once made, the liqueur needs to sit for two weeks to allow the flavors to meld, so plan accordingly. The taste is definitely worth the wait.

PRALINE LIQUEUR

2	cups firmly packed dark brown sugar
1	cup sugar
2½	cups water
4	cups pecan pieces (1 pound), lightly toasted
2	vanilla beans, split lengthwise
4	cups vodka

Combine sugars and water in a medium saucepan; cook over medium-high heat until sugar dissolves. Bring to a boil; reduce heat, and simmer 5 minutes. Place pecans and vanilla beans in a 1-gallon jar. Pour hot mixture into jar; let cool. Add vodka; stir well. Cover tightly; store in a dark place at least 2 weeks at room temperature. Shake jar gently daily.

Pour mixture through a wire-mesh strainer, lined with cheese-cloth, into a bowl; discard pecans and vanilla beans. Pour mixture through a wire-mesh strainer lined with a coffee filter; into a bowl. Change filter often. (Mixture will drip slowly.) Pour mixture into glass bottles. Store at room temperature.

Yield: about 4½ cups liqueur

LABELED BOTTLE

You will need red cardstock, flecked cardstock, craft glue, black permanent fine-point marker, jute twine, bottle, white paint pen, hole punch, wooden star with hole, paintbrush, and white acrylic paint.

1. Cut a 1¾" x 2½" piece from red cardstock. Cut a 1¾" x 2¼" piece from flecked cardstock. Glue flecked cardstock rectangle to red cardstock rectangle to make label.
2. Using marker, write recipe name on label and draw borders on top and bottom of flecked cardstock rectangle.
3. Cut an 18" length of jute twine. Wrap jute twine around top of bottle. Tie knot leaving 4"-long tails.
4. Cut a 1" x 2½" piece from red cardstock to make gift tag. Using white paint pen, write recipient's name on tag. Punch hole in tag.
5. Paint wooden star white. Thread tag and star onto one tail of jute twine. Tie jute twine into knot to secure.

BLISSFUL BITES

This homemade version of a popular candy bar is rolled into balls and drizzled with ribbons of melted chocolate. A shallow wooden box decorated with glass baubles keeps the candies in one layer and makes for an attractive delivery.

COCONUT CANDIES

- ½ cup butter
- 2 cups sifted confectioners sugar
- 3 cups flaked coconut
- ½ cup semisweet chocolate chips

Melt butter in a saucepan over low heat; remove from heat. Stir in sugar and coconut; shape into ¾-inch balls. Chill until firm.

Place chocolate chips in a small heavy-duty resealable plastic bag; seal. Submerge in hot water until chocolate melts. Snip a tiny hole in one corner of bag, and drizzle chocolate over coconut balls. Store in refrigerator.
Yield: about 3½ dozen candies

MOSAIC BOX

You will need wooden box, green paint, assorted marbles, small mirrored tile, craft glue, grout, rubber gloves, sponge, tissue paper, and individual paper candy wrappers.

Allow paint and glue to dry after each application.

1. Paint wooden box using green paint.
2. Referring to photo and using craft glue, attach marbles and mirrored tile to box lid in shape of Christmas tree.
3. Glue marbles along edge of lid.
4. Mix grout with water and green paint until mixture forms

consistency of putty.
5. Wearing rubber gloves, place grout over top of lid until covered. Wipe excess grout from box lid.
6. Using damp sponge, wipe grout from marbles.
7. Referring to photo, line inside of box with tissue paper. Place candies in wrappers and inside box.

BURSTING WITH BANANA FLAVOR

Start the holiday season by sharing slices of this moist coffee cake, elegantly presented on a pretty tray embellished with ribbons and bells. A dusting of confectioners sugar adds a touch of whimsy to this morning treat.

BANANA-SOUR CREAM COFFEE CAKE

1¼	cups sugar, divided
½	cup chopped pecans
1	teaspoon ground cinnamon
½	cup butter, softened
2	eggs
1	cup mashed ripe banana
½	cup sour cream
½	teaspoon vanilla extract
2	cups all-purpose flour
1	teaspoon baking powder
1	teaspoon baking soda
¼	teaspoon salt

Preheat oven to 350 degrees.

In a small bowl, stir together ¼ cup sugar, pecans, and cinnamon; sprinkle half of mixture in a well-greased 12-cup Bundt pan. Set remaining mixture aside.

In a large bowl, beat butter at medium speed of an electric mixer until fluffy; gradually add remaining 1 cup sugar, beating 5 to 7 minutes. Add eggs, 1 at a time, beating just until yellow disappears. Add banana, sour cream, and vanilla, beating at low speed just until blended.

Combine flour, baking powder, soda, and salt; fold into creamed mixture. Pour half of batter into prepared pan; sprinkle with

remaining pecan mixture. Top with remaining batter.

Bake 45 minutes or until a long toothpick inserted in center comes out clean. Cool in pan on wire rack 10 minutes; remove from pan, and cool on wire rack.
Yield: one 10-inch coffee cake

JINGLE BELL CHARGER

You will need thin white string, 24"

of 2"w ribbon, 11 jingle bells, 13" dia. charger, and hot glue gun.

1. Cut several 3" lengths of string. Tie lengths of string along ribbon length at 4" intervals.
2. Tie 1 jingle bell on each string.
3. Referring to photo, glue ribbon to edge of charger at each jingle bell, allowing ribbon to balloon between jingle bells.
4. Trim ribbon ends at an angle to finish.

CORDIALLY YOURS

*T*he combination of blueberry, nutmeg, and cinnamon mix nicely with brandy. A glass decanter tied with decorative cording and a tag is all you need to present this delicious concoction to a friend.

BLUEBERRY SPICE CORDIAL

1	package (16 ounces) frozen blueberries, thawed
1½	cups sugar
½	cup water
6	whole cloves
1	stick (3 inches) cinnamon
1	whole nutmeg, cut in half
3	cups brandy

Combine blueberries, sugar, water, cloves, cinnamon, and nutmeg in a medium saucepan; stir well. Cook over medium-high heat until sugar dissolves. Bring to a boil; reduce heat, and simmer 5 minutes. Remove from heat, and let cool. Pour blueberry mixture into a 2-quart jar. Add brandy; stir well. Cover tightly; store in a dark place at least 2 weeks at room temperature. Shake jar gently once daily.

Pour mixture through a wire-mesh strainer, lined with cheese-cloth, into glass decanters; discard blueberries and spices. Cover tightly. Store at room temperature. *Yield:* about 5 cups cordial

DECORATED DECANTER

You will need a glass decanter with stopper, decorative cording with tassels, blue and white handmade paper, white cardstock, black permanent fine-point marker, glue stick, and hole punch.

1. Referring to photo, tie cording around neck of decanter.
2. Cut a 2½" x 3½" rectangle from white handmade paper. Cut a 2¼" x 3¼" rectangle from blue handmade paper. Tear a 1½" x 3" rectangle from white cardstock. Using marker, write recipe name on white cardstock rectangle.
3. Using glue stick, center and glue white cardstock rectangle to blue handmade paper rectangle. Center and glue these rectangles to white handmade paper rectangle to make gift tag.
4. Punch hole in upper corner of tag. Thread tag onto cording.

SHOW-STOPPING TART

For an elegant tart destined to be talked about, look no further than this chocolate and nut dessert. If you're in a pinch, leave off the white chocolate mixture—the tart will be just as good. Just wrap it in pretty gift paper once set and tie with ribbon. Make sure to include the recipe because you're guaranteed to be asked for it!

DOUBLE CHOCOLATE CASHEW TART

1	crust from a 15-ounce package of refrigerated pie crusts, at room temperature
¾	cup semisweet chocolate chips
1	cup firmly packed brown sugar
½	cup butter
¼	cup honey
3	tablespoons whipping cream
1	tablespoon vanilla extract
2	eggs
2	cups chopped lightly salted cashews
6	squares (1 ounce each) white baking chocolate
3	tablespoons whipping cream
⅓	cup semisweet chocolate chips

Preheat oven to 425 degrees. Roll pie crust into a 12-inch circle. Press into an 11-inch tart pan with removable bottom. Freeze 10 minutes. Bake 8 minutes. Remove from oven and sprinkle chips in bottom of crust. Let stand on wire rack 4 minutes. Spread chocolate over crust with a spatula. Reduce oven temperature to 350 degrees.

Combine sugar, butter, and honey in a medium saucepan; stir well. Cook over medium-high heat until butter melts and sugar dissolves. Bring to a boil; reduce heat, and simmer 2 minutes, stirring occasionally.

Remove from heat; stir in 3 tablespoons whipping cream and vanilla. Cool 15 minutes.

Add eggs, 1 at a time, beating with a wire whisk after each addition. Stir in cashews. Pour cashew mixture into pastry. Bake at 350 degrees for 20 minutes or until set. Let cool completely on a wire rack.

Combine white chocolate and 3 tablespoons whipping cream in a microwave-safe bowl and microwave on HIGH 1 minute, stirring with a whisk until smooth. Pour white chocolate mixture over cooled tart, spreading to edge of pastry.

Melt remaining ⅓ cup semisweet chocolate chips in a heavy-duty resealable plastic bag in microwave on HIGH 1 minute and 30 seconds. Cut a small hole in one corner of bag and pipe melted semisweet chocolate in small circles over white chocolate mixture in center and around edge of tart. Immediately pull tip of a toothpick or knife through each circle, forming small hearts.

Chill 10 minutes or until chocolate mixture is set. To serve, carefully remove sides of tart pan. *Yield:* one 11-inch tart

Note: If you're in a hurry when making this tart, you can leave off the top chocolate layer. It still tastes great and looks equally elegant.

CELLOPHANE WRAP

You will need 20" x 30" sheet of decorative paper, 20" x 30" sheet of cellophane, 2 yds. of 1½"w striped ribbon, pie server, and 45" of 1"w brown ribbon.

1. Place decorative paper over cellophane and place tart on paper. Wrap papers around tart, gathering edges together and securing with striped ribbon.
2. Cover server handle with brown ribbon, crisscrossing to form braid. Leave long ribbon ends. Cut ribbon ends at an angle to finish.

PECAN PLEASURES

A tin embellished with festive trim is the perfect way to give away these sugar-dusted bar cookies.

SNOW-DUSTED PECAN BARS

½   cup butter, softened
¼   cup confectioners sugar
2   cups all-purpose flour
¼   teaspoon salt
1   cup chopped pecans
1   tablespoon vanilla extract
1   tablespoon ice water
Confectioners sugar

Preheat oven to 350 degrees.
In a large bowl, beat butter at medium speed of an electric mixer until fluffy; gradually add confectioners sugar, beating well.

Combine flour and salt; add to creamed mixture, beating at low speed until blended. Stir in pecans, vanilla, and 1 tablespoon ice water.

Shape dough into 4-inch sticks. Place sticks on lightly greased baking sheets.

Bake 12 to 15 minutes or until browned. Roll in confectioners sugar. Store in airtight container 2 weeks, or freeze 2 months.
Yield: about 3 dozen pecan sticks

POM-POM TIN

You will need hot glue gun, 25" of red pom-pom trim, 7" dia. tin with lid, tracing paper, green decorative paper, white cardstock, glue stick, and black permanent fine-point marker.

1. Using hot glue gun, attach pom-pom trim to edge of lid.
2. Trace large tree pattern, page 145, onto tracing paper and cut out. Transfer large tree pattern to decorative paper and cut out. Trace small tree pattern, page 145, onto tracing paper and cut out. Transfer small tree pattern to cardstock and cut out.
3. Using glue stick, adhere decorative paper tree to lid. Center and adhere cardstock tree to decorative paper tree using glue stick. Using marker, write recipe name on cardstock tree to make label.

BOUNTIFUL BREAD

*B*aking bread is a true labor of love and this Touch-of-Wheat Onion Bread will be appreciated for its oniony flavor and soft texture. Pick up an antique bread knife at a flea market and attach a ribbon for an attractive gift.

TOUCH-OF-WHEAT ONION BREAD

2	packages dry yeast
1	tablespoon sugar
1	cup warm water (100 to 110 degrees)
5	cups all-purpose flour, divided
¾	cup whole wheat flour
2	tablespoons dried minced onion
1	tablespoon salt
¼	teaspoon pepper
1	cup milk
3	tablespoons vegetable oil
2	tablespoons spicy brown mustard
1	egg, lightly beaten
1	egg white, lightly beaten
1	tablespoon dried minced onion

In a large bowl, combine yeast and sugar in warm water; let stand 5 minutes. In another large bowl, combine 4 cups all-purpose flour, whole wheat flour, minced onion, salt, and pepper. Add milk, oil, mustard, and egg to yeast mixture. Stir in flour mixture. Gradually stir in enough of remaining 1 cup all-purpose flour to make a stiff dough.

Turn dough onto a lightly

floured surface. Knead 4 or 5 times. Shape into a ball. Place in a large greased bowl, turning once to coat top of dough. Cover and let rise in a warm place (80 to 85 degrees) until doubled in size.

Turn dough onto a lightly floured surface and punch down. Cover dough and let rest 5 minutes. Divide dough in half. Shape each half into a round loaf; place on 2 greased baking sheets. Cover loaves and let rise in a warm place 20 minutes or until doubled in size.

Preheat oven to 375 degrees. Combine egg white and 1 tablespoon minced onion; brush evenly on loaves. Bake 25 minutes or until loaves sound hollow when tapped. Serve warm or transfer to a wire rack to cool completely. Store in an airtight container.
Yield: about 2 loaves bread

BURLAP PACKAGING

You will need burlap, plastic wrap, 1 yd. of 1½"w plaid ribbon, gold paint pen, tin star ornament with hole, and 6" of ¼"w sheer ribbon.

1. Cut two 8" x 36" rectangles from burlap.
2. Pull threads from all sides of rectangles to fray edges.
3. Position two pieces of burlap on table to form plus mark. Wrap bread in plastic wrap and place in center of burlap plus mark.
4. Referring to photo, wrap burlap rectangles to cover bread.
5. Wrap plaid ribbon around burlap to secure and tie into a knot.
6. Using paint pen, write greeting on tin star. Thread star onto sheer ribbon and tie onto knot.

SASSY SAUCE

Sweeten a friend's day with this scrumptious sauce flavored with oranges, pineapple, maraschino cherries, and coconut and used as a dessert topping for cake or ice cream. When the beaded container is empty, use it to store cotton balls, bath salts, or other items.

AMBROSIA SAUCE

1½   cups sugar
1   cup pineapple-orange juice
¼   cup butter
2   teaspoons grated orange zest
4   egg yolks, lightly beaten
½   cup flaked coconut
½   cup chopped pecans, toasted
¼   teaspoon coconut extract
1   can (15 ounces) crushed pineapple, drained
1   jar (6 ounces) red maraschino cherries, chopped

Combine sugar, juice, butter, orange zest, and egg yolks in top of a double boiler; bring water to a boil. Reduce heat to medium-low; cook 15 minutes, stirring constantly. Stir in coconut, pecans, coconut extract, pineapple, and cherries. Serve warm or chilled over ice cream, pound cake, or angel food cake. Refrigerate up to 1 week.
Yield: about 3½ cups sauce

BEADED FRINGE JAR

You will need mason jar with lid, 5" square of red fabric, spray adhesive, purchased red beaded fringe, and hot glue gun.

Allow glue to dry after each application.

1. Unscrew lid of jar and remove insert. Center insert on fabric and trace around it. Cut out fabric circle. Apply spray adhesive to top of insert. Adhere fabric circle to top of insert.
2. Cut a length of beaded fringe to fit around rim of jar lid. Using hot glue gun, glue beaded fringe around rim of lid. Place fabric-covered insert in lid.
3. Pour sauce into jar. Screw lid onto jar. Refrigerate sauce until time to deliver.

CRAVIN' CRANBERRIES

Seasonal cranberries are baked into this mouthwatering coffee cake that sports a crunchy pecan topping. The batter needs to chill for eight hours, so plan to make it a day ahead. For a pretty and practical presentation, deliver the coffee cake in the baking pan for easy reheating. A clear cellophane wrapper dressed with festive ribbon and trims provides a quick glimpse of the gift.

CRANBERRY COFFEE CAKE

¾	cup butter, softened
1	cup sugar
2	eggs
2	cups all-purpose flour
1	teaspoon baking powder
1	teaspoon baking soda
1	teaspoon ground nutmeg
½	teaspoon salt
1	carton (8 ounces) sour cream
1½	cups fresh cranberries
⅓	cup sugar
1¼	cups firmly packed brown sugar
¾	cup chopped pecans
2	teaspoons ground cinnamon

Preheat oven to 350 degrees.

In a large bowl, beat butter at medium speed of an electric mixer until fluffy. Gradually add 1 cup sugar; beat well. Add eggs, one at a time; beat after each addition.

Combine flour, baking powder, baking soda, ground nutmeg, and salt; add to creamed mixture alternately with sour cream, beginning and ending with flour mixture.

Coarsely chop cranberries; press between paper towels to remove excess moisture. Combine cranberries and ⅓ cup sugar; stir well. Pour half of batter into a greased 13 x 9 x 2-inch pan. Sprinkle cranberry mixture evenly over batter.

Combine brown sugar, pecans, and cinnamon. Sprinkle half of pecan mixture evenly over cranberry mixture. Pour remaining batter over pecan mixture. Sprinkle remaining pecan mixture over batter. Cover and chill at least 8 hours. Bake, uncovered, 40 minutes or until a toothpick inserted in center comes out clean. *Yield:* about 15 servings coffee cake

FALL FAVORITE

*J*ars of homemade sweet pumpkin butter topped with a decorative label will be the delight of a holiday breakfast. Spread this tasty butter on thick slices of homemade bread or use it as a topping for pancakes.

PUMPKIN BUTTER

1	can (29 ounces) pumpkin
1½	cups sugar
¾	cup apple juice
2	teaspoons ground cinnamon
2	teaspoons ground ginger
1	teaspoon ground nutmeg
½	teaspoon ground cloves

Combine all ingredients in a large saucepan; stir well. Bring pumpkin mixture to a boil; reduce heat, and simmer 30 minutes or until thickened, stirring frequently. Pour hot pumpkin mixture into hot sterilized jars, filling to ¼-inch from top. Remove air bubbles; wipe jar rims. Cover at once with metal lids, and screw on bands. Cool completely on a wire rack. Store in refrigerator.
Yield: about 5 half-pints pumpkin butter

WRAPPED JAR WITH LABEL

You will need newsprint, rubber band, raffia, photocopy of label design (page 142) on white cardstock, colored pencils, and craft glue.

1. Cut a 5½" dia. circle from newsprint. Place on lid of jar and secure with rubber band. Tie raffia to cover rubber band and into a double knot.
2. Use colored pencils to color label. Cut out label; glue to newsprint circle on top of jar.

KICKED-UP SALSA

This chunky salsa will add a spicy kick to your holiday parties, when served alongside a Mexican style supper or scooped up with corn tortilla chips. Add more peppers if you can take the heat. Not seeding the peppers will also kick the flavor up a notch.

BLACK-EYED PEA SALSA

1	can (15½ ounces) black-eyed peas, drained
2	large plum tomatoes, chopped (about 1½ cups) or 1 can (16 ounces) plum tomatoes, drained and coarsely chopped
1	can (4 ounces) chopped green chiles
2	green onions, chopped
2	canned jalapeño peppers, seeded and chopped
3	tablespoons olive oil
1	tablespoon white wine vinegar
1	clove garlic, minced
½	teaspoon salt
¼	teaspoon pepper

Combine all ingredients in a medium bowl; stir well. Cover and chill at least 8 hours.
Yield: about 3 cups salsa

FABRIC-TOPPED JAR

You will need burlap, paper-backed fusible web, scraps of red and green felt, pint glass jar with lid, 1 yd. of ⅜"w green grosgrain ribbon,

1 yd. of ¼"w red grosgrain ribbon, tortilla chip container, 20" of 1"w red grosgrain ribbon, and 20" of 1½"w green grosgrain ribbon.

1. Cut a 6" square from burlap.
2. Transfer pepper and stem patterns, page 142, to fusible web; cut out. Fuse pepper shape onto small piece of red felt. Fuse stem shape onto small piece of green felt. Cut out shapes along pattern lines. Remove paper backing.

3. Referring to photo, center and fuse pepper and stem felt pieces onto burlap square.
4. Center burlap square on jar lid. Holding ⅜"w green grosgrain ribbon and ¼"w red grosgrain ribbon as one, tie around lid and into a bow.
5. Cover tortilla chip container with burlap. Holding 1"w red grosgrain ribbon and 1½"w green grosgrain ribbon as one, tie around container and into a knot.

SNOW IN THE FORECAST

Rolled in powdered sugar, these cookies resemble miniature snowballs, and they melt in your mouth. The snowflake bag holds a dozen cookies and is held together by a felt snowflake clothespin that can also be used as a refrigerator magnet to hold Christmas cards or photos.

WINTER WEDDING COOKIES

¾	cup butter, softened
½	cup sifted confectioners sugar
2	tablespoons honey
1	teaspoon vanilla extract
2	cups all-purpose flour
¼	teaspoon salt
½	cup finely chopped walnuts

Confectioners sugar

Preheat oven to 325 degrees.

In a large bowl, beat butter at medium speed of an electric mixer until fluffy; add ½ cup confectioners sugar and honey, beating well. Stir in vanilla. Combine flour and salt; add to creamed mixture, mixing until well blended. Stir in walnuts.

Shape dough into 1-inch balls and place 2 inches apart on lightly greased baking sheets. Bake 12 minutes or until lightly browned. Cool slightly on baking sheets. Roll warm cookies in confectioners powdered sugar and cool on wire racks.

Yield: about 3 dozen cookies

SNOWFLAKE GIFT BAG

You will need white spray paint, clothespin, white felt, white paper, silver glitter dimensional paint, craft glue, adhesive-back magnet strip, blue permanent fine-point marker, and blue paper gift bag.

Allow paint to dry after each application.

1. Spray paint clothespin white. Transfer snowflake pattern, page 142, onto felt and onto white paper; cut out. Referring to photo, apply dots of glitter paint to points of snowflakes.

2. Referring to photo, glue felt snowflake to one side of clothespin. Trim magnet strip to fit length of clothespin. Adhere magnet strip to back of clothespin.

3. Write message on front of paper snowflake using marker. Referring to photo, glue paper snowflake to lower front of gift bag.

4. Place cookies inside bag. Fold top of bag to back and secure with snowflake clothespin.

THE PERFECT COMBINATION

*T*his decadent sauce, flavored with cranberries and crème de cassis will be a delicious treat for anyone who receives it. Make sure to use a microwave-safe jar so the recipient can conveniently pop it in the microwave to warm the sauce. Attach a fabric topper to the jar for a nice touch.

CRANBERRY CHOCOLATE SAUCE

1	cup whipping cream
¼	cup sugar
1	cup fresh or frozen cranberries
⅓	cup crème de cassis
6	ounces bittersweet chocolate, chopped

Combine whipping cream, sugar, cranberries, and crème de cassis in a small saucepan. Bring to a boil over medium heat, stirring constantly, until sugar dissolves. Reduce heat, and simmer, uncovered, 12 minutes or until cranberries pop. Remove from heat; add chocolate and stir until smooth (place over low heat if necessary to melt chocolate). Press mixture through a wire-mesh strainer and into a clean glass jar; discard cranberry skins.
Yield: about 2 cups sauce

To Reheat: Place sauce in a saucepan over low heat or cover glass jar with plastic wrap and microwave on HIGH 30 seconds or until smooth. Great as a topping for ice cream or poundcake.

BEAD AND FABRIC JAR TOPPER

You will need fabric, pinking shears, beaded hair rubber band, decorative paper, black permanent fine-point marker, and glue stick.

1. Cut an 8½" dia. circle from fabric using pinking shears.

2. Place circle on top of jar lid. Wrap beaded rubber band around fabric to secure.
3. Cut a 2½" dia. circle from decorative paper to make label. Using marker, write greeting.
4. Using glue stick, center and adhere label to fabric.

Dress up a plain lunch bag and fill it with this flavorful snack—sure to please the nut-lover on your list. These cashews are great party fare and the recipe can easily be doubled or tripled.

HERBED CASHEWS

1   egg white
1   teaspoon Dijon mustard
⅛ teaspoon paprika
2   cups lightly salted cashews
⅓ cup grated Parmesan cheese
1   teaspoon dried Italian seasoning
¼ teaspoon salt

Preheat oven to 300 degrees.
Beat egg white at high speed of an electric mixer until foamy; add mustard and paprika, beating just until blended. Add cashews, stirring to coat. Combine Parmesan cheese, Italian seasoning, and salt; sprinkle over cashews; stirring well.

Spread in a single layer on a lightly greased baking sheet. Bake 25 minutes, stirring occasionally. Cool completely on baking sheet. Store in an airtight container.
Yield: about 2 cups cashews

Note: Cashews may be frozen in an airtight container, up to 1 month.

SCALLOPED BAG

You will need paper bag, pencil, hole punch, 24" of 1½"w ribbon, purchased gift tag, black permanent fine-point marker, and string.

1. Referring to photo, draw a scalloped design along opening of bag using pencil.

2. Fold top of bag down 2".
3. Cut out scalloped design on edge of bag.
4. Punch two holes at top of bag. Thread ribbon through holes and tie into a bow.
5. Write greeting on gift tag using marker and attach to bow using string.

EYE-CATCHING TREATS

*S*urprise a friend with these four-ingredient treats that include the ultimate combination of peanut butter and chocolate. An embellished pie box from the bakery is lined with tissue paper to hold these delectable bars that are sure to do a vanishing act.

CHEWY GRANOLA TREATS

1   package (12 ounces) butterscotch chips (2 cups)
½   cups plus 2 tablespoons creamy peanut butter
4   cups granola
1½   cups candy-coated chocolate pieces

Grease a 13 x 9 x 2-inch pan; line with waxed paper.

Combine butterscotch chips and peanut butter in top of a double boiler; bring water to a boil. Reduce heat to low; cook until chips melt.

Combine granola and chocolate pieces in a bowl; pour butterscotch mixture over granola mixture, stirring to coat. Spread mixture in prepared pan. Cover and chill until firm. Cut into squares.
Yield: about 18 squares

TREE BOX

You will need tracing paper, white pie box, craft knife, cellophane, tape, assorted buttons, rick-rack, craft glue, 1 yd. of 1"w green grosgrain ribbon, yellow paper, and green permanent fine-point marker.

Allow glue to dry after each application.

1. Trace tree and star patterns, page 143, onto tracing paper; cut out. Place box lid upside down. Referring to photo, transfer tree pattern to lower inside portion of lid. Using craft knife, cut out tree shape. Center piece of cellophane over tree shape and securely tape cellophane to inside lid.
2. Turn lid right side up. Referring to photo and using craft glue, glue buttons and lengths of rick-rack to cellophane covering tree.
3. Place bars in box. Replace lid.
4. Referring to photo, tie ribbon around top portion of box and into bow, positioning bow over top of tree. Trim ends of ribbon.
5. For gift tag, transfer star pattern to yellow paper and cut out. Using marker, write recipe name on tag and glue to center of bow, making star appear as if on top of tree.

FOR SANDWICH LOVERS

*J*ingle *your way into a man's heart with a jar of homemade horseradish spread and all the fixin's to make a hearty sandwich. Then place it all neatly into a basket trimmed with bells to announce its arrival. The spread can also be used as a dip or accompaniment for roast beef.*

HORSERADISH SPREAD

2	packages (5.2 ounces each) garlic-and-herb-flavored spreadable cheese
¼	cup plus 2 tablespoons prepared horseradish
1	package (8 ounces) cream cheese, softened
½	cup sour cream
2	tablespoon minced fresh dill

Stir together all ingredients until blended. Cover and chill up to 7 days.
Yield: about 2¾ cups spread

JINGLE BELL JAR AND BASKET OF GOODIES

You will need a basket with handle, gold spray paint, ⅛"w gold ribbon, assorted jingle bells, 1⅜"w plaid ribbon, red excelsior, glass jar with lid, pencil, and food items for basket.

Allow paint to dry after each application.

1. Spray paint basket gold.
2. Cut about ten 6" lengths of ⅛"w gold ribbon. Thread jingle bells onto each ribbon length. Referring to photo and spacing as desired, thread ribbons through basket and attach jingle bells to rim of basket, tying ribbons into bows. Tie a length of 1⅜"w plaid ribbon to each base of basket handle, tying ribbons into bows. Fill basket with excelsior.
3. Spoon spread into jar and replace lid.
4. Tie a length of 1⅜"w plaid ribbon into bow around neck of jar. Thread two medium jingle bells onto a 10" length of ⅛"w gold ribbon. Tie jingle bells onto knot in plaid ribbon bow. Wrap tails of gold ribbon around pencil to curl ribbon.
5. Tuck wrapped sliced roast beef, chewy rolls, chips, bottled soft drinks, and embellished jar of spread into basket.

SNACK ATTACK

Nibblers beware! These crackers will disappear without warning, especially at holiday gatherings. Don't worry though, the recipe makes seven cups, enough for you and your friends to enjoy. A little bit of ribbon transforms an ordinary canister into a special gift container.

CRACKER SNACKERS

⅓   cup vegetable oil
1   clove garlic, thinly sliced
2   tablespoons fresh lemon juice
1   package (10 ounces) oyster crackers
1   pouch (1.2 ounces) Caesar dressing mix (we used Good Seasons Gourmet Caesar)
¼   teaspoon ground black pepper
¼   teaspoon garlic powder
2   tablespoons grated Parmesan cheese

Preheat oven to 300 degrees.
Combine oil, garlic, and lemon juice; let stand 30 minutes. Discard garlic.
Place crackers in a bowl; sprinkle with oil mixture. Combine dressing mix, pepper, and garlic powder. Sprinkle over crackers. Place on jelly-roll pan and bake 15 minutes. Remove from oven and sprinkle cheese over cracker mixture.
Yield: about 7 cups crackers

CHOCOLATE FROM ABOVE

A bake-and-take pan full of turtle cheesecake brownies will seem like a gift from above once you bite into the chewy goodness of chocolate, cream cheese, and caramel. Have a child help with the craft part of the gift, as it only requires cutting and gluing. It makes a perfect well-deserved surprise for a teacher!

TURTLE CHEESECAKE BROWNIES

1	cup butter
4	ounces unsweetened baking chocolate, chopped
2¼	cups sugar
4	eggs, lightly beaten
2	teaspoons vanilla extract
¼	teaspoon salt
1	cup plus 2 tablespoons all-purpose flour
1	cup coarsely chopped pecans
2	packages (3 ounces each) cream cheese, softened
2	tablespoons all-purpose flour
2	eggs
1	jar (12.25 ounces) caramel-flavored topping

Preheat oven to 350 degrees.

In a large saucepan over low heat, melt butter and chocolate; remove pan from heat. Let cool slightly.

Stir in sugar, 4 eggs, vanilla, salt, 1 cup plus 2 tablespoons flour, and pecans, stirring until blended after each addition. Spread half of batter into a 9 x 13-inch disposable pan with lid.

Beat cream cheese at medium speed of an electric mixer 1 minute. Add 2 tablespoons flour, 2 eggs, and caramel topping; beat until smooth. Pour over chocolate batter in pan. Drop remaining chocolate batter, ¼ cup at a time, over cream cheese batter; swirl gently with tip of a knife.

Bake 50 minutes or until brownies begin to pull away from sides of pan. Cool in pan on a wire rack. Cut into 2-inch squares. Store in an airtight container.
Yield: about 2 dozen brownies

Note: If you like chewy brownies, bake only 47 minutes.

ANGEL LID

You will need blue paper; craft glue; tracing paper; pencil; white paper plate; yellow curling ribbon; glue stick; decorative-edge craft scissors; pink, blue, and red decorative paper; white cardstock; and black permanent fine-point marker.

1. Referring to photo, cut blue paper into a cloud shape large enough to cover flat area of plastic lid of aluminum baking pan. Using craft glue, adhere cloud to lid.
2. Trace angel patterns, page 144, onto tracing paper; cut out. Transfer angel patterns onto white paper plate and cut out.
3. Cut 3" length of curling ribbon. Cut length into five or six short pieces and glue one end of each piece to top of head to form hair.
4. Referring to photo, cut two small circles from pink paper to form cheeks. Using glue stick, adhere to angel face. Referring to photo, draw face using marker.
5. Using craft scissors, cut a 2" x 4" rectangle from blue decorative paper, a 1¾" x 3½" rectangle from red paper, and a ¼" x 3" rectangle from white cardstock. Center and glue white rectangle on red rectangle using glue stick. Center and glue red rectangle on blue rectangle using glue stick. Referring to photo, adhere to lid. Using marker, write recipe name on white rectangle.

Cold, wintry nights are a great time to enjoy a mug of piping hot cinnamon mocha; just add hot water and let the taste envelope you. Deliver it to a neighbor in a snowflake-stamped bag with button closures. You can also include a bottle of whipped cream for a fun topping.

CINNAMON MOCHA MIX

1   jar (6 ounces) powdered instant non-dairy creamer
1   cup plus 2 tablespoons sifted confectioners sugar
½   cup instant coffee granules
½   cup cocoa
2   teaspoons ground cinnamon
1   teaspoon vanilla extract
⅛   teaspoon salt

Combine all ingredients in a bowl; mix well. Store in an airtight container.

To serve, place 3 tablespoons mocha mix in a cup. Add ¾ cup boiling water; stir well.
Yield: about 3½ cups mix

SNOWFLAKE BAG

You will need snowflake stamp, white ink pad, blue paper gift bag, white paint pen, hole punch, white string, two ¾" dia. white buttons, and resealable plastic bag.

1. Using snowflake stamp and white ink pad, stamp designs on paper bag. Using paint pen and referring to photo, make dots between designs; allow to dry.

2. Punch two holes 1" from top and 2½" from sides on back side of paper bag. Cut two 6" lengths of string. Thread one string through each hole, knotting string on ends.

3. Referring to photo, sew two buttons 4½" from top and 2½" from sides on front side of paper bag.

4. Place mix in plastic bag and into paper bag. Fold top of bag 2" to front. Wrap each string around buttons to secure.

EGGSTRA SPECIAL STRATA

*T*he gift of convenience shines through in this make-ahead breakfast dish that goes from fridge to oven in a disposable pan and eliminates the need for clean up. Thick slices of this fluffy egg custard would be perfect for breakfast, but even better for a quick lunch or dinner.

SAUSAGE AND CHEDDAR STRATA

1½	pounds ground pork sausage
8	slices (1 inch thick) French bread, cut into 1-inch cubes
1½	cups (6 ounces) shredded Cheddar cheese
8	eggs, lightly beaten
2	cups milk
¾	cup half-and-half
1	teaspoon salt
⅛	teaspoon ground red pepper
⅛	teaspoon ground black pepper

Brown sausage in a large skillet, stirring until it crumbles; drain. Layer bread cubes, sausage, and cheese in a lightly greased 13 x 9 x 2-inch disposable baking dish.

Combine eggs, milk, half-and-half, salt, red pepper, and black pepper; pour over cheese. Cover and chill 8 to 12 hours.

Uncover and bake at 350 degrees 40 to 45 minutes or until set and lightly browned.

Yield: about 8 servings strata

STAR ORNAMENT TAG

You will need tracing paper, ¼ yd. flannel fabric, coordinating color of felt, paper-backed fusible web, black embroidery floss, embroidery needle, batting, and small button.

Refer to Blanket Stitch, page 155, before beginning project.

1. Trace star pattern, page 146, onto tracing paper; cut out. Transfer pattern to flannel and cut out slightly smaller than pattern. Transfer pattern to felt; cut out.

2. Using fusible web, fuse flannel star to felt star.

3. Use six strands of black floss to work *Blanket Stitch* and to secure edges of flannel star.

4. Cut small opening in back of felt star and insert batting to fill space between flannel and felt stars. Stitch felt star opening closed.

5. Stitch button to center of star. Cut 6" length of embroidery floss. Stitch loop of floss to back of star to make hanger.

HOLLY JOLLY BARS

Your next holiday cookie swap just wouldn't be complete without a batch of these yummy bars. Stacked neatly on a decoupaged plate these rich bars boast coffee flavor and bits of English toffee for an intoxicating flavor. Be sure to have extra copies of the recipe on hand for fans of these sweet bars.

GLAZED ALMOND-TOFFEE BARS

1	cup butter, softened
1	cup packed brown sugar
2	cups all-purpose flour
½	teaspoon baking powder
¼	teaspoon salt
1½	cups chopped English toffee-flavored candy bars (about 5), divided
2	packages (2 ounces each) slivered almonds, toasted
1	cup confectioners sugar
2	tablespoons milk
1	tablespoon butter, softened
1	teaspoon vanilla extract
1½	tablespoons instant coffee granules

Preheat oven to 350 degrees. Line a 10½ x 15½-inch jellyroll pan with aluminum foil, extending foil over ends of pan; grease foil. In a large bowl, combine butter and brown sugar. Beat at medium speed of an electric mixer 2 minutes or until creamy. In a small bowl, combine flour, baking powder, and salt. Add flour mixture to butter mixture. Stir in 1 cup chopped toffee and almonds. Spread batter into prepared pan.

Bake 18 minutes or until lightly browned.

Combine confectioners sugar, milk, 1 tablespoon butter, vanilla, and coffee granules in a small bowl. Drizzle over warm bars. Sprinkle with remaining toffee bits. Cool in pan on a wire rack. Use ends of foil to lift from pan. Cut into bars.
Yield: about 30 bars

HOLLY DECOUPAGE PLATE

You will need tracing paper, assorted green decorative papers, red decorative paper, green and red cardstock, clear glass plate (we used a 10" dia. glass plate), sponge paintbrushes, decoupage glue, and gold acrylic paint.

Allow glue to dry after each application.

1. Trace holly leaf patterns, page 147, onto tracing paper and cut out. Transfer holly patterns to assorted green decorative papers and cardstock and cut about 25 holly leaves. Cut circles of various sizes from red decorative paper and cardstock.
2. Turn plate upside down; use paintbrush to apply thin coat of decoupage glue around rim and on bottom of plate. Referring to photo, position holly leaves and berries, face down, onto glue.
3. Apply second coat of glue over all pieces.
4. Paint back side of plate with two coats of gold paint.
5. Add final coat of decoupage glue over gold paint.

RUSTIC CHARM

A tisket, a tasket, a bread-filled basket! Swaddled in cloth, this flavorful rustic country bread contains roasted red peppers and Parmesan cheese and makes for a great sandwich. Since it yields two loaves you can give one away and freeze the other for later. Weave ribbon through a plain basket for an extra special presentation.

PEPPER-PARMESAN COUNTRY BREAD

1	package dry yeast
1	cup warm water (100 to 110 degrees)
1	cup warm milk (100 to 110 degrees)
1	cup grated fresh Parmesan cheese
⅔	cup chopped onion
1	jar (7 ounces) roasted red bell pepper
½	cup yellow cornmeal
2	tablespoons sugar
2	tablespoons olive oil
2	teaspoons salt
2	teaspoons cracked black pepper
3½	cups unbleached all-purpose flour, divided
2	cups whole wheat flour
2	tablespoons yellow cornmeal

In a large bowl, combine yeast, water, and milk; let stand 5 minutes. Add Parmesan cheese, onion, red bell pepper, cornmeal, sugar, olive oil, salt, and pepper to yeast mixture; beat well. Add 2 cups all-purpose flour and whole wheat flour; beat well. Gradually stir in enough remaining all-purpose flour until a soft dough forms. Turn onto a well-floured surface. Knead about 5 minutes or until dough becomes smooth and elastic, using additional flour as necessary. Place in a large greased bowl, turning once to coat top of dough. Cover and let rise in a warm place (80 to 85 degrees) 1 hour or until doubled in size.

Sprinkle 2 tablespoons cornmeal on a large baking sheet; set aside.

Punch dough down, and divide in half. Shape each half into a round loaf; place loaves on prepared baking sheet. Cover and let rise in a warm place 20 minutes or until doubled in size.

Preheat oven to 350 degrees. Bake 30 minutes or until loaves sound hollow when tapped. Remove loaves from baking sheet; let cool on wire racks.
Yield: 2 loaves bread

POINSETTIA PACKAGE

These soft and chewy delights are better than any store-bought version and they require no baking! Cut them into bars or use a cookie cutter to make holiday shapes, and pack in a lined gift box.

NO-BAKE GRANOLA BARS

2½   cups crisp rice cereal
2   cups uncooked quick cooking oats
½   cup raisins
½   cup firmly packed brown sugar
½   cup light corn syrup
½   cup peanut butter
1   teaspoon vanilla extract
½   cup milk chocolate chips

Combine cereal, oats, and raisins in a large bowl; set aside.

Bring brown sugar and syrup to a boil in a small saucepan over medium-high heat, stirring constantly; remove from heat. Stir in peanut butter and vanilla until blended.

Pour peanut butter mixture over cereal mixture, stirring until coated; let stand 10 minutes. Stir in chocolate chips. Press mixture into a lightly greased 13 x 9-inch pan; cool in pan on wire rack. Cut into bars.

Yield: about 15 bars

POINSETTIA PACKAGE TOPPER

You will need tracing paper, red craft foam, hot glue gun, small yellow and white beads, waxed paper, white gift box, 1 yd. of ¾"w ribbon, tape, yellow cardstock, red permanent fine-point marker, and hole punch.

Allow paint and glue to dry after each application.

1. Trace circle and poinsettia leaves patterns, page 148, onto tracing paper; cut out. Using patterns, transfer one circle and three of each leaf patterns onto craft foam, and cut out.
2. Place three largest foam leaves on foam circle with ends meeting in middle. Adhere leaves to circle using hot glue gun.
3. Place three medium foam leaves on top of and between large foam leaves with ends meeting in middle. Adhere medium foam leaves to large foam leaves using hot glue gun.
4. Place three small foam leaves on top of and between medium foam leaves with ends meeting in middle. Adhere small foam leaves to medium foam leaves using hot glue gun.
5. Using hot glue gun, adhere 10 yellow beads and 10 white beads to center of foam leaves.
6. Wrap bars in waxed paper and place inside box. Cut an 18" length of ribbon and wrap lengthwise around box lid, securing ends with tape. Cut a 15" length of ribbon and wrap crosswise around box lid, securing ends with tape.
7. Center and adhere foam poinsettia to box lid using hot glue gun.
8. Cut a 2" x 3" rectangle from yellow cardstock to make gift tag. Using marker, write greeting on tag.
9. Cut a 4" length of ribbon. Punch hole in tag and thread onto ribbon. Tie ribbon length with tag onto ribbon on box lid.

This kid-friendly recipe is perfect for busy little hands. The cookies are rolled into a ball, flattened, and topped with a nut, then delivered in a Rudolph-inspired bag.

CHEESY COOKIE SNACKS

1   cup (4 ounces) shredded Cheddar cheese
½   cup butter or margarine, softened
1   cup all-purpose flour
¼   teaspoon salt
1   cup crisp rice cereal
Assorted nuts (we used pecan halves, cashews, and roasted peanuts)

Preheat oven to 350 degrees.

In a large bowl, stir together cheese and butter until blended. Stir in flour and salt; blend well. Stir in cereal; dough will be stiff.

Shape dough into 1-inch balls; place on an ungreased baking sheet 2 inches apart. Flatten cookies to ½-inch thickness and place a nut on top of each cookie, pressing to adhere.

Bake 15 to 18 minutes. Remove to wire rack to cool.

Yield: about 2 dozen cookies

RUDOLPH SACKS

You will need brown lunch-size paper bag; 20 mm red pom-pom; craft glue; ¾" circular-shaped wiggle eyes; black felt marker; tracing paper; brown craft foam; tape.

1. Glue pom-pom nose to center front of bag; allow to dry. Center and glue eyes above nose; allow to dry. Referring to photo, draw mouth and eyebrows.

2. Trace antler patterns, page 146, onto tracing paper; cut out. Transfer two antler patterns onto brown foam; cut out. Place cookies inside bag. Fold down top of bag towards back about ¾". Tape in place. Referring to photo, glue antlers onto bag.

EDIBLE LOGS

Packaged to resemble a New Year's cracker, this nifty wrapping holds a treat of nougat wrapped in caramel and rolled in pecans.

CARAMEL MARSHMALLOW PECAN LOGS

1	package (16 ounces) confectioners sugar
1¾	cups marshmallow creme
1½	teaspoons vanilla extract
1	package (14 ounces) caramels
3	tablespoons water
2	cups chopped pecans

Combine confectioners sugar, marshmallow creme, and vanilla in a large bowl; stir well. Knead 10 minutes or until smooth. (Mixture will be very dry.) Shape into four 5-inch-long logs. Cover and chill 3 hours.

Unwrap caramels; combine caramels and water in a large skillet. Cook over medium heat until caramels melt; reduce heat to low, and stir until smooth. Working quickly with forks, roll each log in caramel mixture. Roll in pecans, pressing firmly to coat. Cover and chill at least 8 hours. Store in refrigerator.
Yield: about 4 pecan logs

CHRISTMAS CRACKERS

You will need waxed paper, cellophane, tape, red and green raffia, decorative paper, white paper, and red and green permanent fine-point markers.

1. Roll log in waxed paper. Cut a 10" x 12" rectangle from cellophane. Wrap cellophane around log and tape to secure.
2. Cut lengths of raffia. Referring to photo, tie raffia around each end of cellophane.
3. Cut a 4" x 6" rectangle from decorative paper to wrap around log. Tape ends to secure.
4. Cut a 2" x 6" rectangle from white paper. Using red or green marker, write greeting on white rectangle. Center and wrap around decorative paper. Tape ends to secure.

EYE-CATCHING CHEESE

Shaped in a rectangle and powdered with paprika, this cheese brick resembles the real thing in color and weight but tastes much better! The creamy inside is offset by the heat of the paprika and is best served on a hearty cracker. It will definitely be a conversation piece at your next gathering.

CHEESE BRICK

2   blocks (8 ounces each) Cheddar cheese
1   package (8 ounces) cream cheese, softened
1   jar (2 ounces) diced pimentos, undrained
½   cup chopped pecans
1   tablespoon mayonnaise
½   teaspoon garlic salt
½   teaspoon onion salt
¼   cup paprika

Shred Cheddar cheese, and let stand at room temperature 1 hour.

Stir together Cheddar cheese, cream cheese, pimentos, pecans, mayonnaise, garlic salt, and onion salt; shape into a rectangle. Set brick on waxed paper and sift paprika over top, coating evenly. Press any remaining paprika that accumulates on waxed paper onto sides of brick. Chill at least 1 hour. Serve with assorted crackers.
Yield: about 15 to 20 appetizer servings

HANDMADE WRAPPING

You will need brown parchment paper, jute twine, corrugated cardboard, 25" of 1½"w ribbon, yellow hand-made paper, black permanent fine-point marker, and hole punch.

1. Wrap cheese brick in parchment paper. Cut two lengths of jute twine. Referring to photo, tie both ends of parchment paper with lengths of twine.
2. Cut a 2½" x 15" rectangle from corrugated cardboard. Carefully center and wrap cardboard rectangle around cheese brick.
3. Center and wrap ribbon around cardboard rectangle and tie into a bow.
4. Cut a 2" x 3" rectangle from handmade paper to make gift tag. Write recipe name on tag using marker.
5. Cut a length of jute twine. Punch hole in tag and thread onto length of jute twine.
6. Tie length of jute twine with tag around ribbon and into a knot.

*M*erry munchers will definitely enjoy dunking their favorite vegetables into this creamy pesto dip. The dip is also great as a sandwich spread or topping on a baked potato.

PESTO DIP

1	jar (7.5 ounces) pesto
¾	cup sour cream
¼	cup mayonnaise
¼	cup buttermilk

Stir together all ingredients in a medium bowl until blended. Cover and chill. Serve with assorted vegetables.
Yield: about 2 cups dip

JAR AND VEGETABLE BAG

You will need green corrugated paper; handmade paper; double-sided tape; green permanent fine-point marker; brown corrugated paper bag; vegetable-shape beads; hot glue gun; green, red, and brown raffia; red excelsior; and jar with lid.

1. Cut a 4½" x 5½" rectangle from green paper. Tear a 2½" x 3½" rectangle from handmade paper. Using double-sided tape, center and adhere handmade paper rectangle to green paper rectangle to make label.
2. Using marker, write serving instructions on label. Center and adhere label to front of bag.
3. Thread beads onto green raffia and tie in a bow.
4. Using hot glue gun, adhere green raffia bow to top center of paper bag.
5. Fill paper bag to top with red excelsior.
6. Cut lengths of red, green, and brown raffia. Pour dip into jar and seal.
7. Tie raffia lengths around neck of jar into a bow.

CAJUN CRUNCH

An inexpensive basket filled with Spanish moss holds these spicy chips, perfect for snacking when you want something with a little crunch. The chips can be served with salsa, dips, or even homemade gumbo. Extra seasoning is an added bonus, and can be used to coat grilled chicken or fish.

CAJUN SEASONING

- 1½ teaspoons paprika
- 1 teaspoon dried thyme
- ½ teaspoon garlic powder
- ½ teaspoon onion powder
- ½ teaspoon black pepper
- ¼ teaspoon salt
- ¼ teaspoon sugar
- ¼ teaspoon ground red pepper

Combine all ingredients in a small bowl.

CAJUN PITA CHIPS

Split five pitas in half, and cut each half into eight wedges.

Preheat oven to 375 degrees. Arrange pita wedges on greased baking sheets. Coat wedges with cooking spray. Sprinkle 2 teaspoons Cajun Seasoning over wedges. Bake chips 6 minutes or until crisp.

Yield: about 40 chips

WOODEN BASKET

You will need red dimensional paint, woven basket with handle, red raffia, Spanish moss, cellophane, tissue paper, red paper, black permanent fine-point marker, and hole punch.

Allow paint to dry after each application.

1. Using red dimensional paint, write "Joyeux Noël" around rim of basket. (Joyeux Noël is French for Merry Christmas.)
2. Tie lengths of raffia into bows at each side of basket handle. Fill basket with Spanish moss.
3. Wrap chips in cellophane and gather ends. Tie a length of raffia around ends and into a knot. Place cellophane bag inside basket. Wrap container of desired dip in tissue paper. Gather ends at top and tie using raffia. Place dip inside basket.
4. Transfer crawfish pattern, page 149, to red paper and cut out to make gift tag. Using marker, write recipe name on tag. Punch hole in crawfish pincher. Thread crawfish tag onto length of raffia and tie tag onto pita chip bag.

SUPER EASY SAUCE

Going to a holiday gathering? Be sure to bring along a bottle of this sweet and tangy sauce for the hostess. It's super-easy to make; just stir together all four ingredients— no cooking required! Pour it into a unique shaped bottle, add a few accents like ribbon or beads, and your gift is complete. This recipe is easily doubled or tripled, so you can give a bottle to everyone on your list.

ASIAN PINEAPPLE-MUSTARD SAUCE

⅔   cup pineapple preserves
⅓   cup prepared mustard
1   tablespoon teriyaki sauce
1   teaspoon peeled and grated gingerroot

Combine all ingredients in a small bowl; stir well. Store in glass containers in refrigerator. Serve warm, chilled, or at room temperature with ham, chicken, egg rolls, or shrimp.
Yield: about 1 cup sauce

JAZZY JAR

You will need a decorative glass jar with cork stopper; wire cutters; ½ yd. of gold 16-gauge craft wire; needle-nose pliers; small red tassel; red, green, and clear faceted beads; red vellum; gold paint pen; hole punch; and red and gold cording.

1. Using wire cutters, cut a 2" length of wire. Using needle-nose pliers, bend wire into a "U" shape and insert wire ends halfway into top of cork stopper.
2. Referring to photo, tie tassel onto wire loop in stopper.
3. Using wire cutters, cut another 2" length of wire. Referring to photo, thread red, and green, and clear beads onto wire, looping wire after each bead to secure. Referring to photo, twist beaded

wire around wire loop in stopper.
4. Thread several red, green, and clear beads onto remaining craft wire and wrap tightly around neck of jar using needle-nose pliers.
5. Cut a 3" x 4" rectangle from red vellum to make gift tag. Cut off corners of tag. Using paint pen, write recipe name, serving suggestions, and message on tag. Punch hole at top of tag. Thread tag onto length of cording and tie around neck of jar.

TIN OF TWISTS

Flaky pastry, Parmesan cheese, and seasonings make these delectable cheese twists a great accompaniment to soup or salad. For gift-giving, pack them in a decoupaged tin that can be used later as a container for cookies or other treats.

CHEESE TWISTS

½   cup grated Parmesan cheese
¾   teaspoon seasoned pepper
½   teaspoon dried parsley
       flakes
¼   teaspoon garlic powder
1   package (17¼ ounces) puff
       pastry sheets, thawed
1   egg white, lightly beaten

Preheat oven to 450 degrees.
Combine Parmesan cheese, seasoned pepper, parsley flakes, and garlic powder in a small bowl; stir well and set aside.

Unfold one puff pastry sheet. Brush lightly with egg white. Sprinkle 2 tablespoons cheese mixture evenly over surface of pastry sheet; lightly press cheese mixture into pastry sheet. Turn pastry sheet over and repeat procedure.

Cut pastry sheet in half; cut each half into 9 strips (about 1 inch wide). Twist each strip into a tight spiral and place on lightly greased baking sheets.

Repeat procedure with remaining pastry sheet, egg white, and cheese mixture. Bake 16 to 18 minutes or until golden.
Yield: about 3 dozen twists

DECOUPAGED TIN

You will need fruit-design wrapping paper, craft knife, 9" square tin with lid, decoupage glue, sponge paintbrush, gold acrylic paint, large wooden ball with flat bottom, and craft glue.

Allow glue and paint to dry after each application.

1. Cut out fruit designs from wrapping paper using craft knife.

2. Using decoupage glue and sponge paintbrush, paint tin and place fruit cutouts on tin to cover.
3. Smooth out any wrinkles in paper pieces using paintbrush.
4. Apply second coat of decoupage glue over fruit designs. Repeat process until surface is smooth.
5. Paint wooden ball using gold paint. Glue ball to center of lid using craft glue.

Kids will flip for this sweet and fruity tea mix that's infused with strawberry, peach, and orange flavors. It can be served hot or cold all year long. The clever canister is made from one of the empty drink containers and is fun for kids to decorate themselves.

FRUITY-TOOTY TEA MIX

- ¾ cup instant strawberry-lemonade mix
- ¾ cup instant peach iced tea mix
- ⅔ cup instant orange-flavored breakfast drink
- 1 teaspoon ground cinnamon

Combine all ingredients; stir well. To serve, spoon 2 tablespoons mix into a cup. Add 1 cup boiling water; stir well. *Yield:* about 2 cups mix

PAINTED CONTAINER

You will need drink mix canister from recipe, white spray paint, green acrylic paint, sponge, large wooden ball, hot glue gun, red corrugated cardstock, green cardstock, fruit-design decorative paper, glue stick, and black permanent fine-point marker.

Allow paint and glue to dry after each application. Refer to Sponge Painting, page 153, before beginning project.

1. Spray paint canister white. Referring to *Sponge Painting*, paint canister using green paint and sponge, as desired.
2. Paint wooden ball green. Using hot glue gun, adhere wooden ball to top of lid.
3. Cut a 2" x 3" rectangle from corrugated cardstock. Cut a 1¾" x 2¾" rectangle from green cardstock.

4. Cut out fruit shapes from decorative paper. Referring to photo, position fruit cutouts on corrugated rectangle and adhere using glue stick. Place green rectangle on decorated corrugated rectangle and adhere using glue stick.
5. Using marker, write recipe name on green rectangle and draw dots around edges.

PECANS APLENTY

*S*hare *a taste of the Far East this Christmas with our Asian Spiced Pecans. Nestle them in an Asian-inspired sack, complete with chopsticks, for an anytime snack.*

ASIAN SPICED PECANS

2 tablespoons low-sodium soy
  sauce
1 tablespoon tomato paste
2 teaspoons Thai seasoning
  (we used Spice Islands)
1 teaspoon butter, melted
Dash of black pepper
Dash of ground red pepper
4 cups pecan halves
⅛ teaspoon salt

Preheat oven to 350 degrees. Combine soy sauce, tomato paste, Thai seasoning, butter, black pepper, and red pepper in a large bowl, and stir well with a whisk. Add pecan halves; toss well. Spread pecans evenly onto a greased jelly-roll pan. Bake 12 minutes, stirring once. Remove from oven, and sprinkle with salt. Cool completely. *Yield:* about 4 cups pecans

BURLAP BAG

You will need 11" x 30" piece of black burlap, hot glue gun, 18" of 1½"w brocade ribbon, gold paint, wooden bead, resealable plastic bag, 18" of ⅝"w sheer ribbon, embroidery needle, and two chopsticks.

1. Follow Steps 2, 4, and 5 of *Making a Fabric Bag,* page 154,

to make burlap bag.
2. Using hot glue gun, adhere brocade ribbon around top of burlap bag.
3. Paint wooden bead with gold paint; allow to dry.
4. Place pecans in plastic bag;

place inside burlap bag.
5. Tie sheer ribbon around neck of burlap bag and into a knot. Thread bead onto ribbon ends using needle.
6. Slide chopsticks behind sheer ribbon knot.

LIGHT UP A PARTY

This ultra rich, savory cheesecake makes for great party food, especially when spread on crackers or crusty bread. It's easily transported in a decorated hat box that can be later used to store ornaments or other holiday goodies.

CRAB-AND-MUENSTER CHEESECAKE

1¼ cups fine, dry breadcrumbs
3   tablespoons butter, melted
2   packages (8 ounces each) cream cheese, softened
3   eggs
⅔   cup mayonnaise
2   tablespoons all-purpose flour
12   ounces fresh crabmeat, drained and flaked
1¼   cups (5 ounces) shredded Muenster cheese
¼   cup minced fresh chives
1   jar (2 ounces) diced pimento, drained
Garnish: fresh chives (optional)

Preheat oven to 325 degrees. Combine breadcrumbs and butter; stir well. Firmly press crumb mixture in bottom of a 9-inch springform pan; set aside.

In a large bowl, beat cream cheese at high speed of an electric mixer until creamy. Add eggs, 1 at a time, beating well after each addition. Add mayonnaise and flour; mix until blended. Stir in crabmeat, Muenster cheese, chives, and pimento. Pour batter into prepared pan. Bake 1 hour or until center is completely set. Cut around edges with sharp knife to loosen. Cool to room temperature in pan on a wire rack; cover and chill at least 8 hours.

To serve, carefully remove sides of springform pan. Garnish, if desired.

Yield: one 9-inch cheesecake

Note: This cheesecake may be frozen up to 2 weeks. To freeze, cool it completely on a wire rack; carefully remove sides of springform pan, wrap cheesecake airtight, and freeze. Include a gift tag noting that frozen cheesecake should be thawed in refrigerator.

DECOUPAGED PAPIER MÂCHÉ BOX

You will need cardboard; 10" dia. round papier mâché box with lid; green, silver, yellow, red, purple, and blue paint; sponge paintbrush; craft glue; water; handmade decorative tissue paper; wooden bulb beads; black craft wire; hot glue gun; wooden knob; brown cardstock; red permanent fine-point marker; and hole punch.

Allow paint and glue to dry after each application.

1. Cut a 2½" x 3½" rectangle from cardboard. Round corners of rectangle to make gift tag. Paint box, lid, and tag using green paint.
2. Using sponge paintbrush, apply glue and water to outside of box, lid, and tag.
3. While glue and water are still wet, mold tissue paper onto box, lid, and tag to cover.
4. Referring to photo, paint base of bulbs using silver paint and paint bulbs a variety of colors.
5. Thread bulbs onto wire. Using hot glue gun, adhere bulbs to edge of lid.
6. Paint knob using silver paint and glue to center of lid using hot glue gun. Referring to photo, thread three bulbs onto wire and wrap wire around knob.
7. Cut a 2" x 2¼" rectangle from cardstock. Write recipe name and greeting on rectangle using marker. Center and adhere to tag using hot glue gun. Punch hole in tag and thread onto a length of wire. Tie wire to knob on lid.

Crab & Muenster
Cheesecake
*Throw in
Fridge!
Enjoy! JC

CHRISTMAS CHOWDER

*T*he warmth of the holiday
season is embedded in this creamy
soup that sports two kinds of corn
and a hint of heat. A clamp-top
canister is all you need for
delivery!

PEPPER-CORN CHOWDER

6	slices bacon
1	medium onion, finely chopped
2	stalks celery, thinly sliced
1	teaspoon minced jalapeño pepper
2	medium red potatoes, peeled and cubed
2	cups frozen whole kernel corn, thawed
2	cups half-and-half
1	cup milk
1	can (8¾ ounces) cream-style corn
1	teaspoon beef-flavored bouillon granules
¾	teaspoon salt
¼	teaspoon sugar
1	bay leaf, crumbled
1	cup chopped sweet red pepper
2	teaspoons butter, melted

Cook bacon in a large skillet until crisp; remove bacon, reserving drippings in skillet. Crumble bacon and set aside. Sauté onion, celery, and jalapeño pepper in drippings, stirring constantly, until tender.

Transfer sautéed vegetables to a large saucepan; add potato, corn, half-and-half, milk, cream-style corn, bouillon granules, salt, sugar, and bay leaf. Bring to a boil; reduce heat and simmer, uncovered, 25 to 30 minutes or until potato is tender.

Sauté red pepper in butter in a small skillet over medium heat until tender. Stir into soup. Let cool slightly; pour into container. *Yield:* about 7½ cups chowder

RIBBON-LACED CANISTER AND LADLE

You will need airtight canister, hot glue gun, 20" of 1½"w gingham ribbon, 20" of ½"w Christmas tree trim, photocopy of star gift tag, page 147, on white cardstock, red permanent fine-point marker, raffia, and ladle.

Allow glue to dry after each application.

1. Using hot glue gun, adhere gingham ribbon around canister. Referring to photo, adhere trim around bottom of ribbon.
2. Cut out star gift tag. Using marker, draw border around edges of gift tag and write recipe name on gift tag.
3. Punch hole in tag. Thread gift tag and ladle onto length of raffia. Tie raffia around canister and into a knot.

SCRUMPTIOUS SCONES

A bountiful basket filled to overflowing with melt-in-your-mouth Cheddar Scones start anyone's day off right. Add Yuletide pizazz to a plain basket with a little ribbon, wired berries, and greenery.

CHEDDAR SCONES

2	cups all-purpose flour
2	teaspoons baking powder
½	teaspoon salt
½	teaspoon dried thyme
¼	teaspoon ground red pepper
¼	cup plus 2 tablespoons butter
½	cup (2 ounces) shredded sharp Cheddar cheese
⅔	cup buttermilk
2	teaspoons Dijon mustard
1	tablespoon butter, melted

Sesame seeds

Preheat oven to 425 degrees.
In a large bowl, combine flour, baking powder, salt, thyme, and red pepper; stir well. Cut in butter with a pastry blender until mixture is crumbly. Stir in cheese. Combine buttermilk and mustard; stir well and add to flour mixture, stirring just until dry ingredients are moistened.

Turn dough out onto a lightly floured surface and knead lightly 4 or 5 times. Pat dough into a 7-inch circle on a greased baking sheet. Using a sharp knife, cut circle into 8 wedges; separate wedges slightly. Brush tops of wedges with melted butter; sprinkle with sesame seeds. Bake 15 minutes or until golden.
Yield: about 8 scones

MARDI GRAS IN A BAG

This flavorful gift includes Creole Blend, along with recipes for Jambalaya and a dip that use the blend. Packed in a ribbon-adorned bag, your friends will be dancing in the streets after they taste this spicy mix!

CREOLE BLEND

¼ cup dried parsley flakes
3 tablespoons dried celery flakes
3 tablespoons dried thyme
2 tablespoons dried oregano
2 tablespoons freeze-dried chives
1 tablespoon black peppercorns
1 teaspoon paprika
4 bay leaves
3 dried red chile peppers

Place all ingredients in a food processor or coffee grinder; process until finely ground.
Yield: about ½ cup blend

SPICY OLIVES

An assortment of olives infused with chiles and garlic makes a festive house-warming gift, especially when presented in a beautiful jar with a garland of chiles. Save any remaining oil to use in salad dressings.

PEPPER-MARINATED OLIVES

6	cups assorted olives (Greek, Italian, and Spanish)
2	limes, thinly sliced
1	head fresh garlic, separated into cloves and halved
15	small dried chiles
1	tablespoon freshly ground pepper
4	cups olive oil

Combine olives, limes, garlic, chiles, and pepper in a large glass container; pour olive oil over mixture, stirring well. Cover and refrigerate up to two months, stirring occasionally. Let stand at room temperature 1 hour before serving. To serve, remove and discard lime slices. Transfer olive mixture to a serving bowl using a slotted spoon. Reserve remaining olive oil for other uses.
Yield: about 6 cups olives

FESTIVE JAR

You will need raffia, dried red chile peppers, a large glass jar with cork stopper, handmade paper, gold paint pen, decorative paper, and hole punch.

1. Cut 1 yd. of raffia. Beginning 6" from one end of raffia length, tie raffia several times around one pepper. Repeat, leaving 1" between each pepper, until pepper ribbon is long enough to wrap around neck of jar. Tie pepper ribbon around neck of jar and into a bow.
2. To make gift tag, cut a 3" square from handmade paper and rip sides to create uneven edges. Using gold paint pen, write recipe name on tag. Punch hole in corner of tag.
3. Cut a 2" x 4" rectangle from decorative paper and fold in half lengthwise to make another tag. Using gold paint pen, write serving suggestions inside folded tag. Punch hole in corner of tag through fold.
4. Cut a length of raffia. Thread both tags onto raffia and tie around neck of jar and into a bow.

115

Dress up shortbread cookies with a quick dip in chocolate and a sprinkling of nuts for a super-easy treat. A tin decoupaged with colorful handmade paper and topped with a decorative tag makes a festive gift.

SHORTBREAD DIPPERS

8 ounces chocolate candy coating, chopped
1 cup chopped cashews, almonds, or peanuts
3 packages (5.3 ounces each) shortbread cookies

Stirring occasionally, melt chocolate coating in top of double boiler over simmering water.

Spread nuts in a shallow dish. Dip 1 edge of each cookie into melted coating, covering no more than half of cookie. Sprinkle coated edge with chopped nuts. Place on waxed paper, and let stand until coating is firm and dry. *Yield:* about 32 cookies

Note: If you don't have a double boiler, set a bowl over a small saucepan filled with simmering water.

PAPER TIN

You will need maroon handmade paper, white cardstock, glue stick, black permanent fine-point marker, decoupage glue, sponge paintbrush, hot glue gun, and holly stickers.

Allow glue to dry after each application.

1. Cut a 2¼" x 3¼" rectangle from handmade paper. Cut a 2" x 3" rectangle from cardstock. Center and adhere cardstock rectangle to paper rectangle, using glue stick, to make label. Using marker, write recipe name on label.
2. Using paintbrush, apply decoupage glue to tin and lid.
3. Tear handmade paper into small pieces and place on tin and lid to cover.
4. Center and adhere label to lid using hot glue gun. Adhere holly stickers to four corners of label.

This sweet muffin batter is studded with tangy cranberries and laced with orange peel for an elegant breakfast treat. A basket trimmed with fringe makes a lovely presentation. For an extra touch that takes just seconds, trim the edges of the fabric lining the basket using pinking shears.

CRANBERRY-ORANGE MUFFINS

1½   cups all-purpose flour
½   cup sugar
2   teaspoons baking powder
½   teaspoon salt
¾   cup milk
¾   cup vegetable oil
1   egg
2   teaspoons grated orange zest
¾   cup sweetened dried
     cranberries
1   tablespoon sugar

Preheat oven to 425 degrees.

Grease and flour a muffin pan or line pan with paper liners.

In a large bowl, combine flour, sugar, baking powder, and salt. In a small bowl, beat together milk, oil, and egg. Gently stir egg mixture into flour mixture. Fold in orange zest and cranberries.

Spoon into prepared muffin cups, filling about three-fourths full. Sprinkle 1 tablespoon sugar over batter in muffin cups. Bake 16 minutes or until a toothpick inserted in center comes out clean. Serve warm or cool completely.

Yield: about 1 dozen muffins

FOUR CHEESE CHEESECAKE

Surprise your favorite holiday hostess with this appetizing treat that boasts four cheeses. To easily place and remove cheesecake from the decorated box, simply place it on sheets of overlapping horizontal and vertical plastic wrap to use as a lever.

APPETIZER CHEDDAR CHEESECAKE

1	cup soft breadcrumbs, toasted
⅓	cup grated Parmesan cheese
¼	cup plus 1 tablespoon butter, melted
3	packages (8 ounces each) cream cheese, softened
3	cups (12 ounces) shredded Cheddar cheese
1	cup small-curd cottage cheese
⅔	cup chopped green onions
3	tablespoons canned jalapeño peppers, seeded and chopped
2	tablespoons milk
1	clove garlic, minced
¾	teaspoon chili powder
4	eggs

Garnishes: fresh Cilantro leaves and red bell pepper slices

Preheat oven to 350 degrees. Grease bottoms and sides of an 8-inch springform pan. Combine breadcrumbs, Parmesan cheese, and butter in a small bowl; stir well. Coat bottom of greased pan with breadcrumb mixture. Bake 8 to 10 minutes or until set; set aside. Position knife blade in a large capacity food processor bowl; add cream cheese. Process 1½ minutes or until smooth. Add Cheddar cheese, cottage cheese, green onion, jalapeño pepper, milk, garlic, and chili powder; process 2 minutes, scraping sides of processor bowl occasionally. Add eggs, one at a time, processing after each addition just until well blended. Pour cheese mixture into prepared pan. Bake at 325 degrees 1 hour or until almost set. Turn oven off, partially open oven door, and let cheesecake cool 1 hour. Transfer to a wire rack. Remove sides of springform pan. Garnish with cilantro and red bell pepper slices. Cut cheesecake into thin wedges and serve with wheat crackers.
Yield: one 8-inch cheesecake

HOLLY BOX

You will need tracing paper, green and red cardstock, decorative-edge craft scissors, red pen, craft glue, 9"-dia. papier mâché box, hole punch, red raffia, and 1 yd of sheer ribbon.

1. Trace holly leaf patterns, page 148, onto tracing paper and cut out. Transfer holly leaf patterns onto green cardstock and cut out using craft scissors. Repeat to make approximately 20 holly leaves. Reserve one leaf for gift tag.
2. Trace berry pattern, page 148, onto tracing paper and cut out. Transfer berry pattern onto red cardstock and cut out. Repeat to make approximately 14 berries.
3. Using red pen and referring to photo, outline and detail holly leaves.
4. Referring to photo, glue holly leaves, varying sizes, and berries around box creating a garland. Glue holly leaves and berries in center of box lid.
5. Using red pen, write recipe name on holly leaf reserved for gift tag.
6. Using hole punch, cut hole in one end of holly leaf tag. Cut a length of raffia. Thread tag onto raffia. Tie ribbon around lid into bow. Tie tag onto bow.

119

RED AND WHITE SHOWSTOPPER

A chewy crust is spread with raspberry preserves then sprinkled with white chocolate and a buttery crumb topping for a mouth-watering bar. Santa might even enjoy a tin of these instead of cookies with a cold glass of milk as he's making his Christmas Eve rounds.

CHEWY RASPBERRY AND WHITE CHOCOLATE BARS

2½   cups all-purpose flour
1   cup sugar
½   teaspoon ground
        nutmeg
1   cup chopped walnuts
⅔   cup butter, softened
2   eggs
1   jar (10 ounces) raspberry
        preserves
1   bar (4 ounces) white
        chocolate, chopped

Preheat oven to 350 degrees.

In a large bowl, combine flour, sugar, and nutmeg. Add walnuts, butter, and eggs to flour mixture; beat until crumbly. Reserve 1½ cups crumb mixture; press remaining crumb mixture into bottom of a lightly greased 9-inch square baking pan.

Spread preserves over crust leaving a ½-inch margin around edges; sprinkle chocolate over preserves. Sprinkle reserved crumb mixture over chocolate. Bake 40 to 45 minutes or until lightly browned. Cool completely in pan on a wire rack. Cut into bars.

Yield: about 20 bars

DECOUPAGED AND PAINTED TIN

You will need tin with lid, decorative paper, decoupage glue, sponge paintbrush, coordinating colors of paint, glue stick, label, and green permanent fine-point marker.

Allow glue and paint to dry after each application.

1. Measure length around tin and cut paper 1" longer than tin. Wrap paper around tin, folding excess paper inside tin, and adhere using decoupage glue and sponge paintbrush.

2. Paint lid using paint in colors that coordinate with decorative paper.

3. Cut a 4" circle from paper. Center and adhere paper circle to lid using glue stick.

4. Center and adhere label to circle on lid using glue stick. Using fine-point marker, write recipe name on label.

*E*levate the Christmas spirit this season by bringing a jug full of Cinnamon-Spiced Cider to your next event. Save the jug that the apple cider comes in, as it doubles as the container to hold the recipe.

CINNAMON-SPICED CIDER

1	gallon apple cider
1	cup red cinnamon candies
1	orange, thinly sliced
2	tablespoons frozen lemonade concentrate

Combine all ingredients in a Dutch oven. Bring to a boil; reduce heat, and simmer, uncovered, 30 minutes, stirring occasionally. Let cool and strain through a funnel into gift container. Serve hot or cold.
Yield: about 1 gallon cider

To Reheat: Place desired amount of cider into a pan and warm on the cooktop.

DECORATED CIDER JUG

You will need a clean, empty gallon cider jug from recipe, 3 yds. of 1½"w plaid ribbon, hot glue gun, dried greenery, and cinnamon sticks.

1. Referring to photo, wrap a length of ribbon around jug handle to cover. Secure ends of ribbon to handle using hot glue gun.

2. Referring to photo, wrap length of ribbon around cider jug and tie ribbon into knot, leaving long tails. Trim ribbon ends at angle. Using hot glue gun, adhere greenery and cinnamon sticks to jug at knot.

3. Following *Making a Bow,* page 152, tie remaining plaid ribbon into a multi-looped bow and attach onto knot, greenery, and cinnamon sticks.

4. Pour cooled cider into jug and seal with top.

121

CAN DO CHUTNEY

Two favorites of the season—succulent dates and juicy oranges—come together in this versatile chutney. Use the chutney as a topping for pork or as a spread on a variety of crackers. Tuck inside a bell-trimmed coffee can.

DATE-ORANGE CHUTNEY

2	oranges
4	cups sugar
5½	cups cider vinegar (5% acidity)
1½	teaspoons dried crushed red pepper
1	pound pitted dates, chopped
2	medium onions, chopped
2½	cups raisins

Grate zest from oranges; set zest aside. Peel and discard pith from oranges; chop orange sections, discarding seeds.

Combine sugar, vinegar, and crushed red pepper in a large Dutch oven. Cook over low heat, stirring constantly, until sugar dissolves. Add chopped orange, dates, onion, raisins, and half of grated orange zest to Dutch oven. Bring to a boil; reduce heat, and simmer, uncovered, 2 hours or until mixture is very thick, stirring occasionally. Remove from heat, and stir in remaining orange zest.

Spoon hot chutney into hot jars, filling to ½ inch from top. Remove air bubbles; wipe jar rims. Cover at once with metal lids, and screw on bands. Process in boiling-water bath 10 minutes. Let chutney stand at room temperature at least 2 weeks before serving. Refrigerate after opening.
Yield: about 7 half-pints chutney

PAINTED COFFEE CAN

You will need coffee can, black spray paint, ice pick, 16-gauge wire, needle-nose pliers, green cotton fabric, 1½"w wired ribbon, silver thread, two jingle bells, white cardstock, craft glue, and black permanent fine-point marker.

Tearing cotton fabric as described creates the soft irregular fabric edges seen in photo.

1. Paint can using black spray paint.
2. Using ice pick, punch hole in can ½" from rim. Punch another hole on opposite side of can from first hole.
3. Cut a 12" piece of wire. Slide one end of wire through one hole in can and loop wire using pliers to secure in hole. Repeat on opposite side.
4. Tear a 14" square from fabric. Place fabric around jar of chutney and place inside can.
5. Tie ribbon around can and into a bow.
6. Cut two 4" lengths of thread. Thread one jingle bell onto each length. Tie thread with bell to ribbon.
7. Cut a 2½" x 4" rectangle from white cardstock. Fold cardstock in half to make gift tag. Cut a 2½" x ½" length of ribbon and glue to the front of tag. Using marker, write greeting on tag.

SNOWMAN DELIVERY

When it comes to holiday sweets, chocolate fudge usually tops the list and this recipe is no exception. A rich chocolate fudge is topped with crushed peppermint candies for a flavor explosion. Friends will delight in receiving this treat, especially when given in a painted pencil box embellished with snowmen.

PEPPERMINT FUDGE

2½	cups sugar
½	cup butter or margarine
1	can (5 ounces) evaporated milk
1	package (12 ounces) semisweet chocolate chips (2 cups)
1	jar (7 ounces) marshmallow creme
¾	cup finely crushed hard peppermint candy
1	teaspoon vanilla extract

Additional crushed hard peppermint candy

Line a greased 9-inch square pan with aluminum foil, allowing foil to extend over edges. Grease foil.

Combine sugar, butter, and milk in a medium saucepan. Bring to a boil over medium heat; boil 5 minutes, stirring constantly. Remove from heat; add chocolate chips and marshmallow creme, stirring until smooth. Stir in ¾ cup crushed peppermint candy and vanilla.

Spread mixture into prepared pan; sprinkle with additional crushed peppermint candy. Cool

in pan. To serve, remove fudge from pan, using edges of foil to lift out. Cut fudge into squares; remove foil.
Yield: about 3 pounds fudge

SNOWMAN PENCIL BOX

You will need blue spray paint, pencil box, white paint, small and large round sponges, toothbrush, acrylic paints in assorted colors, gift tag, and waxed paper.

Allow paint to dry after each application. Refer to Sponge

Painting, page 153, before beginning project.

1. Spray paint box blue.
2. Referring to *Sponge Painting* and using white paint and sponges, paint snowmen on box and on gift tag.
3. Dip toothbrush bristles in white paint and flick bristles to splatter white paint on box.
4. Referring to photo, paint details on snowmen using assorted colors of paint.
5. Write greeting on gift tag and attach to box with ribbon. Line box with waxed paper and place fudge inside.

*T*he old saying "easy as pie" clearly rings true with this recipe. It's blended with the touch of a button and then poured into a pie shell for a quick homemade gift. The time you save can be spent decorating the pie box with handmade paper and a glitter glue snowflake design.

BLENDER PECAN PIE

⅔   cup sugar
½   cup light corn syrup
2   tablespoons butter, melted
1   teaspoon vanilla extract
½   teaspoon salt
2   eggs
1   cup pecan halves
1   unbaked 9-inch pastry shell

Preheat oven to 400 degrees.
Combine sugar, corn syrup, butter, vanilla, salt, and eggs in container of an electric blender; process until smooth, stopping once to scrape down sides. Add pecans; pulse 1 or 2 times or until pecans are coarsely chopped. Pour mixture into pastry shell.

Bake 15 minutes. Reduce oven temperature to 325 degrees; bake 35 minutes or until set, shielding edges with aluminum foil to prevent excessive browning, if necessary. Cool on a wire rack.
Yield: one 9-inch pie

SNOWFLAKE BOX

You will need blue handmade paper, 12" square bakery box, double-sided tape, craft glue, white glitter, white rhinestones, and tissue paper.

1. Tear blue paper into a 9½" square. Adhere paper square to box lid using tape.
2. Referring to photo and using glue, draw snowflake on lid.
3. Sprinkle glitter on glue and shake off excess.
4. Using craft glue and referring to photo, glue rhinestones at points of snowflake and along box sides.
5. Line inside of box with tissue paper.

SPREAD SOME CHEER

*E*veryone's favorite condiment gets kicked up a notch as peppers and onions are added to a jar of mustard. It's delicious on soft pretzels, and depending on your mood, you can use spicy or sweet mustard. Put it right back into the original mustard jar, and jazz up the jar lid.

PEPPERY ONION MUSTARD

1	cup minced onion
¾	cup minced sweet red pepper
¼	cup sugar
½	teaspoon dried crushed red pepper
1	cup prepared mustard

Combine onion, minced red pepper, sugar, and dried red pepper in a medium saucepan. Cook uncovered, stirring occasionally, over medium heat until sugar dissolves. Cook uncovered, stirring frequently, an additional 20 minutes or until liquid is evaporated. Remove from heat and cool. Stir in mustard. Store in glass containers in refrigerator. Serve with hamburgers, hot dogs, ham, or use as a sandwich spread.
Yield: about 1½ cups mustard

PEPPER JAR

You will need glass jar with airtight lid; a photocopy of label design

(page 150) on yellow cardstock to fit jar lid; yellow, red, and green cardstock; red, green, and black permanent fine-point markers; craft glue; tracing paper; hole punch; and red and green raffia.

1. Referring to photo, color in pepper design on label using red and green markers. Outline pepper using black marker. Write recipe name around edges of yellow cardstock circle using black marker.
2. Using craft glue, adhere yellow cardstock label onto jar lid.
3. To make gift tag, trace pepper and stem patterns, page 150, onto tracing paper; cut out. Cut a 3" x 4" rectangle from yellow cardstock. Transfer pepper pattern onto red cardstock and cut out. Transfer stem pattern onto green cardstock and cut out. Referring to photo, glue pepper and stem onto tag. Trim yellow cardstock around pepper shape.
4. Outline pepper and stem using black marker. Write serving suggestions in center of pepper. Punch hole at top of tag. Cut lengths of red and green raffia. Thread tag onto raffia and tie around neck of jar and into a bow.

126

MUFFIN MANIA

A button-adorned basket of warm Chocolate-Banana Muffins makes a delicious holiday breakfast for busy shoppers, especially when spread with a pat of warm butter.

CHOCOLATE-BANANA MUFFINS

¾	cup butter, softened
⅓	cup sugar
⅓	cup firmly packed brown sugar
2½	cups mashed ripe banana
3	eggs
2	cups sifted cake flour
1½	teaspoons baking soda
½	teaspoon salt
1½	cups shreds of wheat bran cereal, crushed
1	cup chopped walnuts
1	package (6 ounces) semisweet chocolate chips

Preheat oven to 350 degrees. Line a muffin pan with paper muffin cups or grease and flour muffin pan.

In a large bowl, beat butter at medium speed of an electric mixer until fluffy; gradually add sugars, beating well. Add banana; beat well. Add eggs, one at a time, beating well after each addition.

In a small bowl, combine flour, baking soda, salt, and wheat bran; add to banana mixture, stirring just until moistened. Stir in walnuts and chocolate chips. Let batter stand 5 minutes. Fill muffin cups about three-fourths full. Bake 20

minutes or until a toothpick inserted in center comes out clean. Cool 5 minutes in pans; remove, and cool completely on wire racks. *Yield: about 24 muffins*

LINED BASKET

You will need white felt, basket with handle, assorted buttons, hot glue gun, purchased gift tag, green and black permanent fine-point markers, tape, and 42" of 1½"w ribbon.

1. For liner, cut a 17" x 20" rectangle from white felt. Fold rectangle in half. Cut shape from felt as seen on page 149.
2. Place felt liner in basket and fold any excess felt on inside of basket.
3. Using hot glue gun and referring to photo, adhere buttons around edge of felt.
4. Outline gift tag using green marker. Using black marker, write recipe name on tag. Tape tag to basket handle. Tie ribbon around basket handle and into a bow.

Health enthusiasts will go nuts over a jar of either homemade cashew or peanut butter that contains no additives or preservatives. Include an assortment of graham crackers along with the decorative jar and handmade tag.

PICK-A-NUT BUTTER

2	cups roasted, unsalted cashews or peanuts
1	tablespoon peanut oil
½	teaspoon salt

Process all ingredients in a food processor until well blended. Store in an airtight container in refrigerator up to 2 weeks.
Yield: about 1¼ cups butter

NUT JAR

You will need clamp-top jar, acorn stickers, tracing paper, brown cardstock, corrugated cardstock, craft glue, gold glitter, black permanent fine-point marker, and jute twine.

1. Place stickers on sides and top of jar.
2. Trace acorn and squirrel patterns, page 150, onto tracing paper; cut out. Transfer acorn pattern onto brown cardstock. Transfer squirrel pattern onto corrugated cardstock. Cut out.
3. Referring to photo, place glue on top third of acorn shape. Sprinkle glitter onto glue.

4. Overlap acorn shape on squirrel shape and adhere using glue to make gift tag. Using marker, write recipe name on tag.
5. Tie jute twine around jar and top of tag and into a knot.

128

CAKE LOOK-ALIKE

This eye-catching box, decorated like a prize-winning cake, holds an abundance of chocolate cake mix cookies, guaranteed to satisfy anyone's sweet tooth. Be careful where you set the box, someone might try to sneak a slice and be very surprised!

CAKE MIX COOKIES

1	package (18.25 ounces) devil's food cake mix
1	egg
½	container (8 ounces) frozen whipped topping, thawed
1	cup chopped pecans (optional)
½	cup confectioners sugar

Preheat oven to 350 degrees. Combine cake mix, egg, and whipped topping, stirring well (dough will be sticky). Stir in chopped pecans, if desired. Dust hands with confectioners sugar, and shape dough into ¾-inch balls. Coat balls with confectioners sugar and place 2 inches apart on ungreased baking sheets. Bake 12 minutes or until done; remove to wire racks to cool.
Yield: about 5 dozen cookies

CAKE MIX COOKIE BOX

You will need plastic knife, sheetrock mud, 8½" dia. papier mâché box, brown spray paint, shellac, pecans, and hot glue gun.

Allow sheetrock mud, paint, and shellac to dry after each application.

1. Using plastic knife, spread sheetrock mud on box as if icing cake. Repeat process on box lid. Keep box and box lid separate so mud won't seal together.
2. Spray paint box and box lid brown to resemble chocolate icing.
3. Paint shellac on pecans. Using hot glue gun, adhere pecans to top of box lid.
4. Stack cookies inside box.

SWEET SPREAD

This stunning cheesecake spread will be the envy of the dessert table at your next Christmas party. Sponge paint a pie box from the bakery and top it with a bow to conceal this chocolate show-stopper.

BLACK FOREST CHEESECAKE SPREAD

2   packages (8 ounces each) cream cheese, softened
⅔   cup ricotta cheese
¼   cup confectioners sugar
½   teaspoon ground cinnamon
4   squares (1 ounce each) semisweet chocolate, melted and cooled
1   cup maraschino cherries, drained and minced
1   package (2¼ ounces) sliced almonds, toasted and finely chopped
6   chocolate wafer cookies, crushed
Garnishes: whipped cream, maraschino cherries, sliced almonds

Line bottom and sides of a 7-inch springform pan with heavy-duty plastic wrap; set aside.

Beat cheeses at medium speed of an electric mixer until creamy; gradually add confectioners sugar and cinnamon, beating well. Slowly add melted chocolate, beating at low speed until blended. Stir in minced cherries and chopped almonds.

Spoon chocolate mixture into prepared pan, pressing with back of large spoon to remove any air bubbles. Cover and chill at least 8 hours.

Unmold cheesecake spread onto serving plate. Dip knife into hot water; smooth surface of spread with knife. Press cookie crumbs into sides of spread. Garnish, if desired. Serve at room temperature with chocolate wafer cookies.
Yield: about 4 cups spread

SPONGE-PAINTED HOLLY BOX

You will need tracing paper, pop-up craft sponge, green and red paint, box with lid, pencil, ⅝"w ribbon, hot glue gun, green paper, silver paint pen, hole punch, and ⅛"w ribbon.

Allow paint to dry after each application. Refer to Sponge Painting, page 153, before beginning project.

1. Trace small and large holly leaf patterns, page 147, onto tracing paper; cut out. Transfer small holly leaf pattern to craft sponge and cut out. Wet sponge to expand and squeeze out excess water.
2. Using sponge and green paint and referring to *Sponge Painting*, paint holly leaves in shape of wreath onto center of box lid. Overlap leaves as necessary to make wreath look full.
3. Using pencil eraser and red paint and referring to photo, dot paint onto wreath to make berries.
4. Tie ⅝"w ribbon into bow and trim ends. Using hot glue gun and referring to photo, adhere bow to box lid.
5. To make gift tag, transfer large holly leaf pattern to green paper and cut out. Use silver paint pen to write message on tag. Punch hole in top of tag. Thread tag onto ⅛"w ribbon and tie to bow on box lid.

131

*S*prinkle *a dash of Classic French Flavors to season a pork roast for the holiday table, or use it to make French Herb Butter. Place the mix in a small fabric sack, trimmed with pinking shears and tied with a bow, to spread cheer to a worthy recipient.*

CLASSIC FRENCH FLAVORS

12	bay leaves
¼	cup dried thyme
¼	cup dried parsley flakes
2	tablespoons dried tarragon
2	tablespoons dried basil
1	teaspoon black peppercorns
1	teaspoon dried orange peel

Place all ingredients in a food processor or coffee grinder; process until finely ground. *Yield:* about ⅓ cup seasoning blend

French Herb Butter:

In a small bowl, combine ½ cup softened butter and ¾ teaspoon Classic French Flavors until blended.

FABRIC BAG

You will need ⅛ yd. of fabric, thread to match fabric, pinking shears, resealable plastic bag, rubber band, 1 yd. of grosgrain ribbon, purchased gift tag, and black permanent fine-point marker.

1. Cut a 5" x 16" piece of fabric. Follow Steps 1, 2, and 5 of *Making a Fabric Bag,* page 154, to make bag.
2. Trim top of bag with pinking shears.

3. Place seasoning blend in plastic bag and place inside fabric bag.
4. Fasten rubber band around bag to secure, leaving 3" fabric at top. Tie ribbon over rubber band and into a bow.

MAGNIFICENT MIX

A new twist on an old favorite, these blond brownies boast golden raisins, coconut, and no chocolate! For a clever gift presentation, layer all ingredients in a clear container, using a funnel. This recipe makes enough for two gifts, so bake a batch for yourself.

BLOND BROWNIE MIX

1	package (16 ounces) light brown sugar
2	cups self-rising flour
1½	cups chopped pecans
1½	cups flaked coconut
1	cup golden raisins

Layer ingredients in order listed in an airtight 2-quart glass container. Store in a cool, dry place up to 2 months.
Yield: about 8⅓ cups mix

To prepare brownies: Beat 3 eggs, ½ cup butter, softened, and 1 tablespoon vanilla extract at medium speed of an electric mixer until blended; gradually add Blond Brownie Mix, beating until blended. Spoon into a greased and floured 13 x 9-inch pan. Bake at 350 degrees for 20 minutes; reduce oven temperature to 325 degrees, and bake 25 more minutes. Cool in pan on a wire rack. Cut into squares.
Yield: about 16 brownies

JAR WITH LABEL

You will need a 2-quart jar with lid, 25" of 1½"w ribbon, gold paper, cream paper, decorative-edge craft scissors, glue stick, black permanent fine-point marker, red raffia, and hole punch.

1. Place mix in jar as directed in recipe. Replace lid.
2. Tie ribbon length around jar and into a bow.

3. Cut a 4" x 6" rectangle from gold paper. Cut a 3½" x 5½" rectangle from cream paper using craft scissors. Center and adhere cream rectangle to gold rectangle using glue stick to make label.
4. Write recipe name and baking instructions on label using marker. Punch hole in label and thread onto a length of raffia. Tie raffia around knot in bow.

A GEM OF A COOKIE

A bright red tin decorated with gingerbread men announces that the Christmas season has arrived, especially when filled with mouth-watering cookies topped with chocolate. Be sure to let the chocolate cool on the cookies before you stack them, otherwise they'll smear. And don't forget to save a few for Santa!

WHITE CHOCOLATE-ALMOND GEMS

¾	cup butter, softened
4	squares (1 ounce each) white chocolate, melted and cooled
¾	cup sugar
¾	cup firmly packed brown sugar
1	egg
¼	cup milk
1	teaspoon vanilla extract
¼	teaspoon almond extract
2¼	cups all-purpose flour
1	teaspoon baking powder
¼	teaspoon salt
2¼	cups finely chopped almonds, divided
36	white chocolate and milk chocolate kisses
36	milk chocolate kisses with almonds

In a large bowl, beat butter and white chocolate at medium speed of an electric mixer until fluffy; add sugars, beating well. Add egg, milk, vanilla, and almond extract; beat well.

Combine flour, baking powder, and salt; add to butter mixture, beating well. Stir in ½ cup chopped almonds. Cover and chill 1 hour.

Preheat oven to 375 degrees.

Shape dough into 1-inch balls; roll in remaining almonds. Place 2 inches apart on lightly greased baking sheets. Bake 8 minutes. Unwrap kisses, and press 1 kiss into top of each cookie; bake 2 additional minutes. Cool 1 minute on baking sheets; cool completely on wire racks.

Yield: about 5 dozen cookies

Note: Keep dough in refrigerator between batches, as it will be easier to shape into balls. This recipe makes at least enough for two gifts with a few morsels left over for the cook.

GINGERBREAD TIN

You will need tracing paper; plain red tin; brown, red, black, and white paint; small paintbrush; 68" of 1½"w ribbon; brown cardstock; black permanent fine-point marker; hole punch; and string.

Allow paint to dry after each application.

1. Trace gingerbread man and woman patterns, page 147, onto tracing paper; cut out. Transfer gingerbread patterns around sides of tin, as desired. Transfer one gingerbread pattern on lid.
2. Using brown paint and paintbrush, paint gingerbread patterns.
3. Using white, black, and red paints and paintbrush, paint details on gingerbread men and women, referring to photo.
4. Write message on lid using white paint and paintbrush.
5. Tie ribbon around tin and into a bow.
6. Cut a 3" x 4" piece of cardstock. Fold cardstock in half to make gift tag. Using marker, write greeting on tag. Punch hole in top corner of tag through fold. Thread tag onto length of string and tie to handle of tin.

HOMEMADE WAFFLES AND SYRUP

To warm a neighbor on a wintry morning, surprise her with a pouch of homemade waffle mix and a bottle of homemade maple syrup that the whole family can enjoy. Remember to include instructions for making the waffles and advise to use the syrup in a timely fashion, as it only keeps for two weeks.

PECAN WAFFLES

2½ cups all-purpose flour
1 tablespoon plus 1 teaspoon baking powder
¾ teaspoon salt
1½ tablespoons sugar

Combine flour, baking powder, salt, and sugar in a large bowl. Mix well. Store in a cool, dry place up to 2 months.

To prepare waffles: Combine 2 eggs, 2½ cups milk, and ¾ cup oil; add to flour mixture, stirring with a wire whisk just until dry ingredients are moistened. Stir in ½ cup finely chopped pecans. Cook in a preheated, oiled waffle iron according to manufacturer's directions, or until golden.
Yield: about 16 (4-inch) waffles

HOMEMADE MAPLE SYRUP

1 cup water
2 cups sugar
½ teaspoon maple flavoring

Bring water to a boil in a small saucepan; add sugar and flavoring. Boil 2 minutes, stirring constantly; remove from heat. Serve warm, chilled, or at room temperature. (Store leftover syrup in an airtight container in refrigerator about two weeks.)
Yield: about 2 cups syrup

POURER

You will need glass jar, cardstock, glue, artificial maple leaves stems, and 1 yd ½"w ribbon.

1. Referring to photo, glue cardstock label to jar. Use ribbon to tie maple leaves to neck of jar.

DRAWSTRING POUCH

You will need fabric, thread to match, large safety pin, ribbon, decorative-edge craft scissors, green cardstock, gold paint pen, seasonal stickers, hole punch, and large resealable plastic bag.

1. Cut two 9" x 12" pieces from fabric. With right sides facing and using a ½" seam allowance, stitch sides and bottom of bag.
2. Fold top edges back and 3" down toward bottom of bag. Match side seams and pin in place. Beginning and ending at one side seam, topstitch around folded area of bag. Repeat to create ½"-wide casing for drawstring.
3. Turn bag right side out. Cut stitches at each side seam within casing. Attach safety pin to one end of ribbon and thread through casing around bag.
4. Using craft scissors, cut a 4" x 6" rectangle from green cardstock for recipe card. Write recipe on card using paint pen. Decorate card corners with stickers. Punch hole in one corner of card.
5. Pour waffle mix into plastic bag and seal. Place plastic bag inside fabric pouch and draw opening closed. Thread card onto ribbon and tie into a bow.

NUTTY NIBBLERS

A breeze to assemble, these tangy cheese wafers are best when paired with a glass of wine and are excellent for holiday nibblers or as a topping for creamy soups. The snowflake container adds a bit of whimsy to this thoughtful gift that a cheese lover would surely appreciate. Throw in a bottle of wine, if you'd like.

BLUE CHEESE WALNUT WAFERS

1	package (4 ounces) blue cheese, softened
½	cup butter, softened
1¼	cups all-purpose flour
⅛	teaspoon salt
⅓	cup finely chopped walnuts

Position knife blade in a food processor; add blue cheese, butter, flour, and salt. Process until blended, stopping once to scrape down sides. (Mixture will be sticky). Transfer mixture to a bowl; stir in walnuts. Cover and chill 5 minutes. Divide dough in half. Shape each portion into an 8-inch log. Wrap in heavy-duty plastic wrap; chill 1 hour or until firm.

Preheat oven to 350 degrees.

Slice dough into ¼-inch slices; place on ungreased baking sheets. Bake at 350 degrees 12 minutes or until lightly browned. Let cool on wire racks. Store in airtight container up to 1 week.

Yield: about 4½ dozen wafers

SNOWFLAKE CONTAINER

You will need blue plastic container with lid, assorted snowflake stickers, white paint pen, 5 white pipe cleaners, and 40" of ¾"w white ribbon.

1. Referring to photo, apply snowflake stickers to container and lid. Using paint pen, paint dots around container and lid between snowflakes.
2. Cut three, 5" lengths from pipe cleaners. Place two pipe cleaners on a flat surface and form an "X."

Place a pipe cleaner across middle of "X," referring to figure on page 151. Twist three stems where they meet to make six-point snowflake.
3. Cut six, 2" lengths from pipe cleaners. Twist a 2" length at midpoint of each snowflake point.
4. Cut six, 1¼" lengths from pipe cleaners. Twist a 1¼" length at end of each snowflake point.
5. Tie ribbon around container and into a knot. Place pipe cleaner snowflake in center of knot and knot again.

PATTERNS

STAR BAG
(page 14)

star pattern

HOLLY TIN
(page 31)

holly leaf pattern

CELLOPHANE BAG
(page 30)

tree
pattern

PATTERNS *(continued)*

CROSS-STITCHED ORNAMENT

(page 18)

X	DMC	COLOR
⊙	906	apple green
△	321	Christmas red
◉	741	tangerine orange
•	602	fuchsia pink
⊠	996	aqua blue

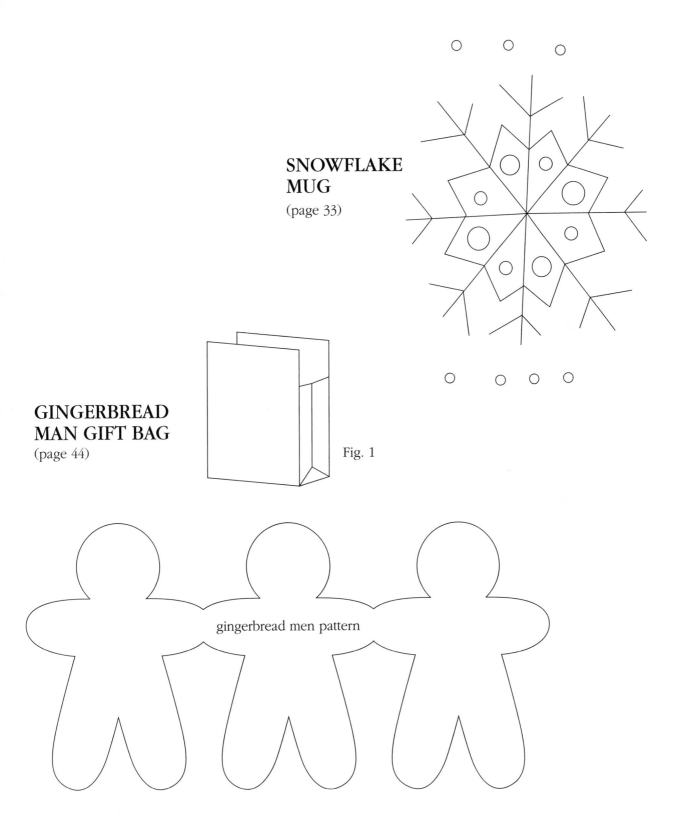

SNOWFLAKE MUG

(page 33)

GINGERBREAD MAN GIFT BAG

(page 44)

Fig. 1

gingerbread men pattern

PATTERNS *(continued)*

HOLLY STENCIL BAG
(page 62)

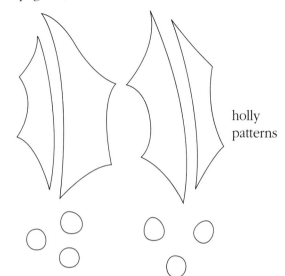

holly
patterns

WRAPPED JAR WITH LABEL
(page 84)

label

SNOWFLAKE GIFT BAG
(page 86)

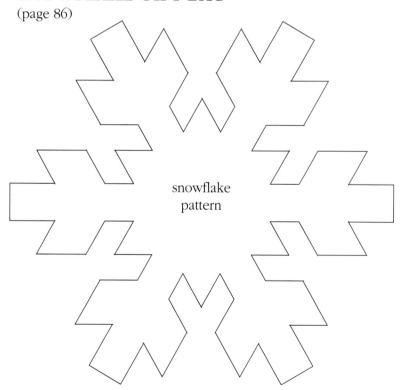

snowflake
pattern

FABRIC-TOPPED JAR
(page 85)

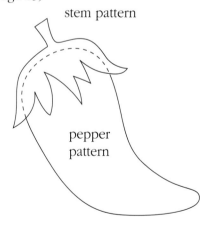

stem pattern

pepper
pattern

Publishers grant permission to the owner of this book to photocopy the tags and labels on these pages for personal use only.

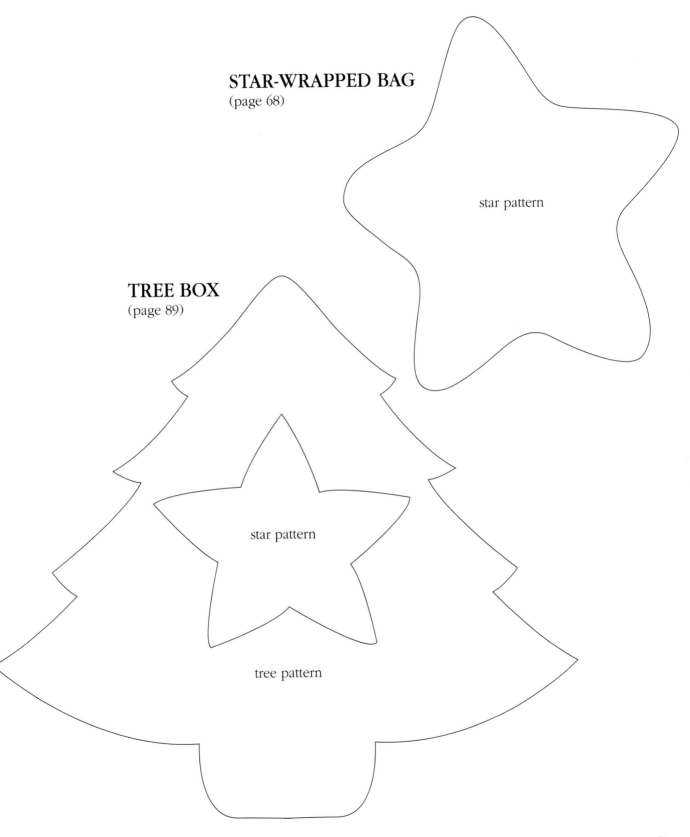

STAR-WRAPPED BAG
(page 68)

star pattern

TREE BOX
(page 89)

star pattern

tree pattern

PATTERNS *(continued)*

ANGEL LID
(page 92)

angel patterns

POM-POM TIN

(page 80)

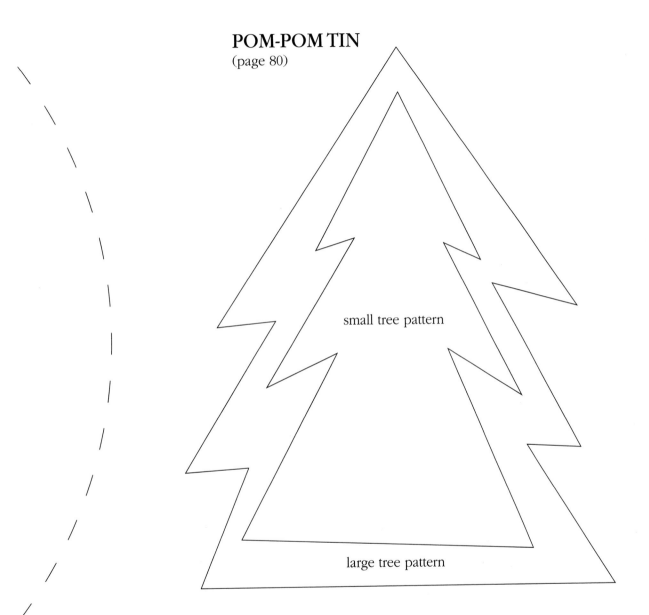

small tree pattern

large tree pattern

PATTERNS *(continued)*

RUDOLPH SACKS
(page 100)

**STAR
ORNAMENT
TAG**

(page 95)

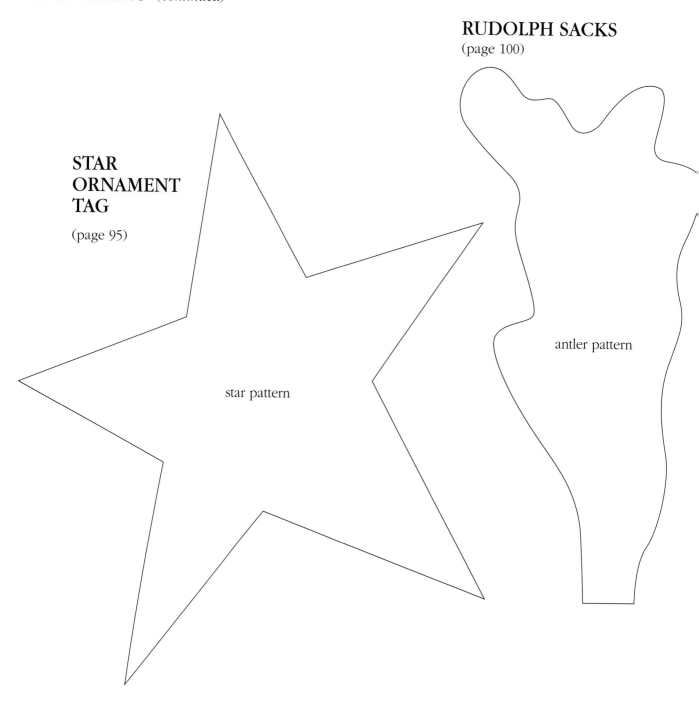

star pattern

antler pattern

Publishers grant permission to the owner of this book to photocopy the tags and labels on these pages for personal use only.

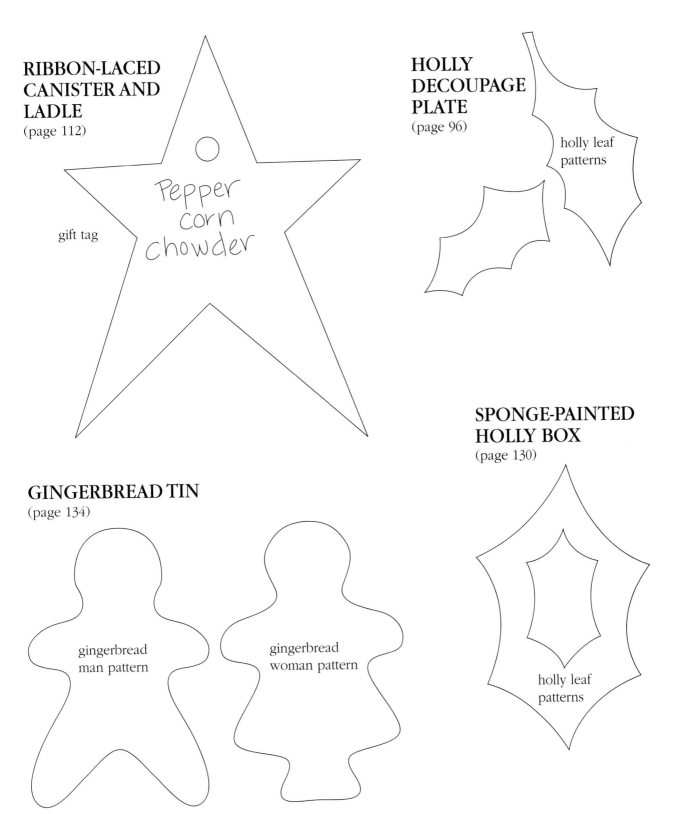

RIBBON-LACED CANISTER AND LADLE
(page 112)

Pepper corn chowder

gift tag

HOLLY DECOUPAGE PLATE
(page 96)

holly leaf patterns

SPONGE-PAINTED HOLLY BOX
(page 130)

holly leaf patterns

GINGERBREAD TIN
(page 134)

gingerbread man pattern

gingerbread woman pattern

147

PATTERNS *(continued)*

HOLLY BOX
(page 118)

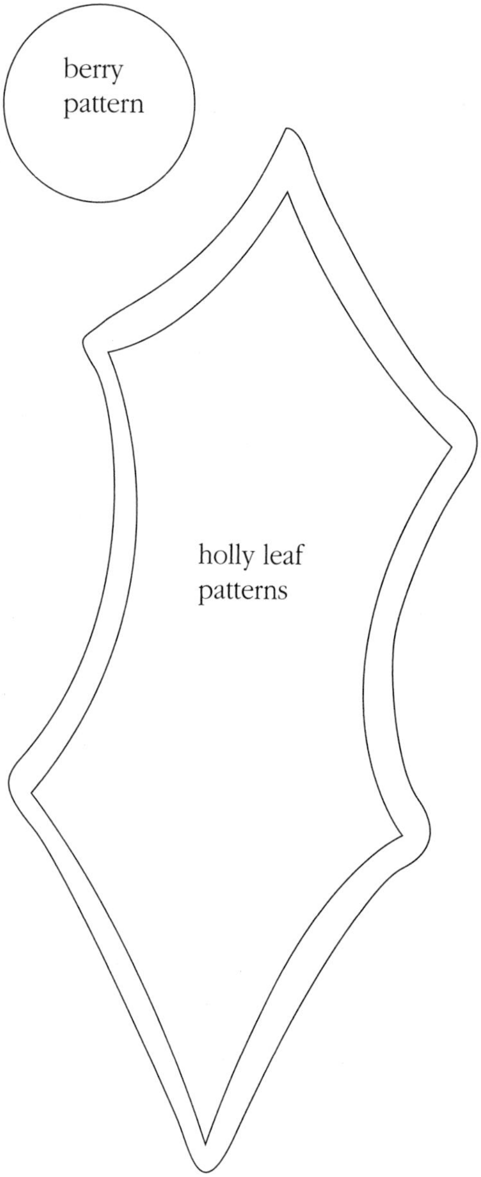

berry
pattern

holly leaf
patterns

POINSETTIA PACKAGE TOPPER
(page 98)

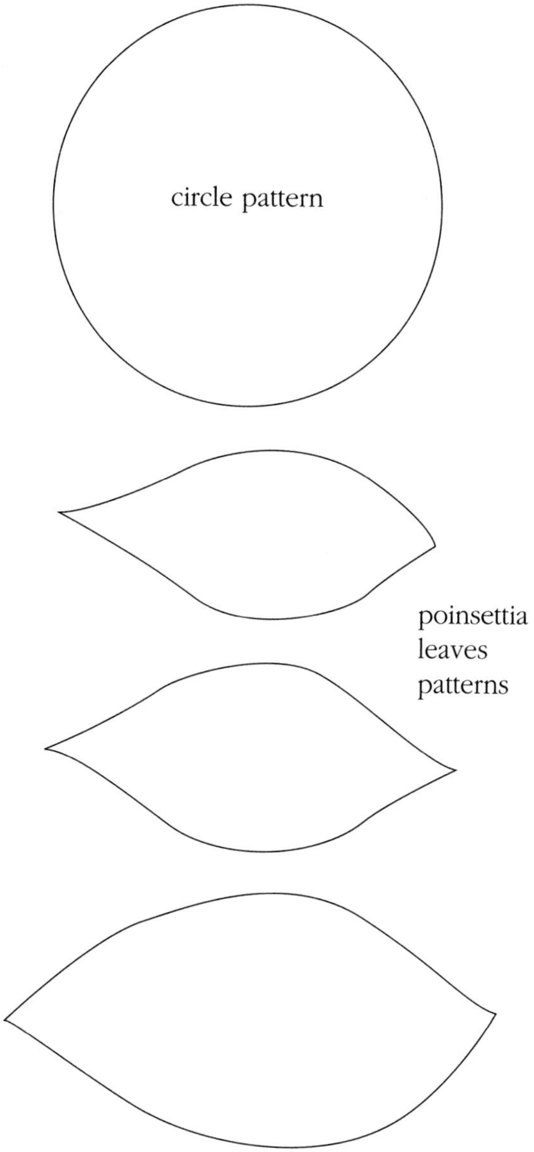

circle pattern

poinsettia
leaves
patterns

Publishers grant permission to the owner of this book to photocopy the tags and labels on these pages for personal use only.

WOODEN BASKET

(page 104)

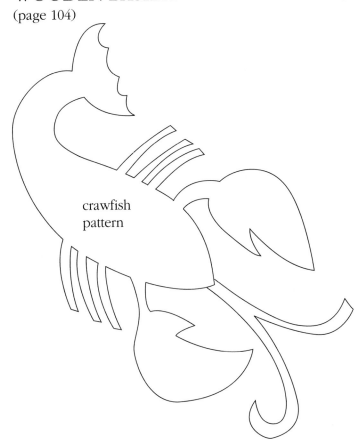

crawfish
pattern

LINED BASKET

(page 127)

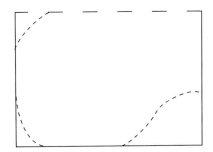

PATTERNS *(continued)*

NUT JAR
(page 128)

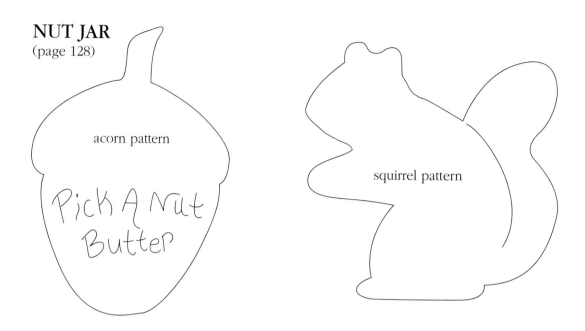

acorn pattern

Pick A Nut
Butter

squirrel pattern

PEPPER JAR
(page 126)

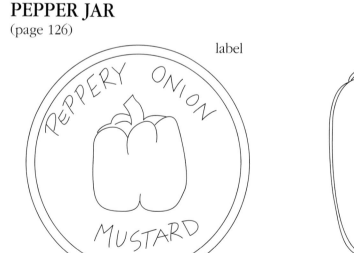

label

PEPPERY ONION

MUSTARD

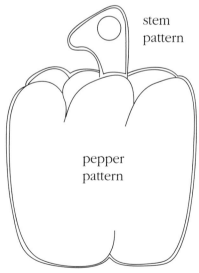

stem
pattern

pepper
pattern

Publishers grant permission to the owner of this book to photocopy the tags and labels on these pages for personal use only.

SNOWFLAKE CONTAINER

(page 138)

GENERAL INSTRUCTIONS

About The Paper We Used

For many of the projects in this book, we used white and colored paper. There are a variety of papers for these projects available at copy centers or crafts stores. When selecting paper, choose one that is suitable in weight for the project. We used copier paper, card and cover stock, construction paper, and handmade paper.

About Adhesives

Refer to the following list when selecting adhesives. Carefully follow the manufacturer's instructions when applying adhesives.

CRAFT GLUE: Recommended for paper, fabric, wood, and floral items. Dry flat or secure with clothespins or straight pins until glue is dry.
FABRIC GLUE: Recommended for fabric or paper items. Dry flat or secure with clothespins or straight pins until glue is dry.
HOT-OR LOW-TEMPERATURE GLUE GUN AND GLUE STICKS: Recommended for paper, fabric, and floral items; hold in place until set. Dries quickly. Low-temperature glue does not hold as well as hot glue but offers a safer gluing option.
CRAFT GLUE STICK: Recommended for small, lightweight items. Dry flat.
SPRAY ADHESIVE: Recommended for adhering paper or fabric items. Dry flat.
RUBBER CEMENT: Recommended for adhering paper to paper; dries quickly.

DECOUPAGE GLUE: Recommended for applying fabric or paper pieces to smooth surfaces.
HOUSEHOLD CEMENT: Used for ceramic and metal items; secure until set.

Making Patterns

When entire pattern is shown, place tracing paper over pattern and trace pattern; cut out. For a more durable pattern, use a permanent pen to trace pattern onto stencil plastic; cut out.

When only half of pattern is shown (indicated by blue line on pattern), fold tracing paper in half and place fold along blue line of pattern. Trace pattern half. Turn folded paper over and draw over traced lines on remaining side of paper. Unfold paper and cut out pattern. For a more durable pattern, use a permanent pen to trace pattern half onto stencil plastic; turn stencil plastic over and align blue line with traced pattern half to form a whole pattern. Trace pattern half again; cut out.

When patterns are stacked or overlapped, place tracing paper over pattern and follow a single colored line to trace pattern. Repeat to trace each pattern separately onto tracing paper.

Making Appliqués

When tracing patterns for more than one appliqué, leave at least 1" between shapes on web.

To make a reverse appliqué, trace pattern onto tracing paper, turn traced pattern over, and follow all steps using traced pattern.

When an appliqué pattern contains shaded areas, trace along entire outer line for appliqué indicated in project instructions. Trace outer lines of shaded areas for additional appliqués indicated in project instructions.

1. Trace appliqué pattern onto paper side of web. (Some pieces may be given as measurements.) Cutting about ½" outside drawn lines, cut out web shape.
2. Follow manufacturer's instructions to fuse web shape to wrong side of fabric. Cut out shape along drawn lines.

Making A Bow

Loop sizes given in project instructions refer to the length of ribbon used to make one loop.

1. For first streamer, measure desired length of streamer from one end of ribbon; twist ribbon between fingers (Fig. 1).

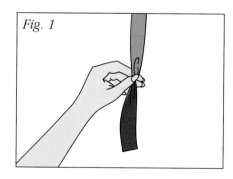

Fig. 1

2. Keeping right side of ribbon facing out, fold ribbon to front to form desired-size loop; gather ribbon between fingers (Fig. 2).

Fig. 2

Fold ribbon to back to form another loop; gather ribbon between fingers (Fig. 3).

Fig. 3

3. If a center loop is desired, form half the desired number of loops; then loosely wrap ribbon around thumb and gather ribbon between fingers (Fig. 4). Continue to form loops, varying size of loops as desired, until bow is desired size.

Fig. 4

4. For remaining streamer, trim ribbon to desired length.

5. To secure bow, hold gathered loops tightly. Fold a length of floral wire around gathers of loops. Hold wire ends behind bow, gathering all loops forward; twist bow to tighten wire. Arrange loops and trim ribbon ends as desired.

Painting Techniques

A disposable foam plate makes a good palette.

TRANSFERRING A PATTERN:
Trace pattern onto tracing paper. Using removable tape, tape pattern to project. Place transfer paper, coated side down, between project and tracing paper. Use a pencil or an old ballpoint pen that does not write to transfer outlines of base coat areas of design to project. (Press lightly to avoid smudges and heavy lines that are difficult to cover.) If necessary, use a soft eraser to remove any smudges.
PAINTING BASE COATS:
Use a medium round brush for large areas and a small round brush for small areas. Do not overload brush. Allowing to dry between coats, apply several thin coats of paint to project for adequate coverage.
TRANSFERRING DETAILS:
To transfer detail lines to design, replace pattern and transfer paper over painted base coat; use pencil or old pen to lightly transfer detail lines onto project.

ADDING DETAILS:
Use a permanent pen to draw over detail lines.
SPATTER PAINTING:
Cover work area with paper and wear old clothes when spatter painting. Before painting item, practice painting technique on scrap paper.
1. Place item on flat surface.
2. Mix 2 parts paint to 1 part water. Dip toothbrush in diluted paint and pull thumb firmly across bristles to spatter paint on item. Repeat as desired. Allow to dry.
SPONGE PAINTING:
Use an assembly-line method when making several sponge-painted projects. Place project on a covered work surface. Practice sponge-painting technique on a sheet of scrap paper until desired look is achieved. Paint projects with first color and allow to dry before moving to next color. Use a clean sponge for each additional color.

For allover designs, dip a dampened sponge piece into paint; remove excess paint on a paper towel. Use a light stamping motion to paint item.

For painting with sponge shapes, dip a dampened sponge shape into paint; remove excess paint on a paper towel. Lightly press sponge shape onto project. Carefully lift sponge. For a reverse design, turn sponge shape over.

GENERAL INSTRUCTIONS *(continued)*

Making A Fabric Bag

Bag may be hand-stitched, machine-stitched, glued, or fused. Follow instructions below unless given specific measurements or different instructions in craft instructions.

1. To determine width of fabric needed, add ½" to desired finished width of bag. To determine length of fabric needed, double desired finished height of bag; add 1½". Cut a piece of fabric the determined measurements.
2. Matching right sides and short edges, fold fabric in half; finger press folded edge (bottom of bag). Using a ¼" seam allowance, sew sides of bag together.
3. For bag with flat bottom, match each side seam of fold line at bottom of bag; sew across each corner 2" from point (Fig. 1).

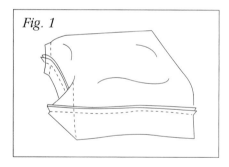

Fig. 1

4. Press top edge of bag ¼" to wrong side; press again to ½" to wrong side and stitch in place.
5. Turn bag right side out.

Making A Basket Liner

For liner with an unfinished edge, cut or tear a fabric piece ¼" larger on all sides than desired finished size of liner. Fringe edges of fabric piece ¼" or use pinking shears to trim edges.

For liner with a finished edge, cut a fabric piece ½" larger on all sides than desired finished size of liner. Press edges of fabric piece ¼" to wrong side; press ¼" to wrong side again. Stitch in place.

Cross Stitch

BACKSTITCH (B'ST)
For outline or details, Backstitch (shown in chart and color key by colored straight lines) should be worked after the design has been completed (Fig. 1).

Fig. 1

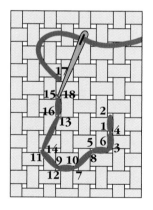

COUNTED CROSS STITCH (X)
Work one Cross Stitch for each colored square on chart. For horizontal rows, work stitches in two journeys (Fig. 2).

Fig. 2

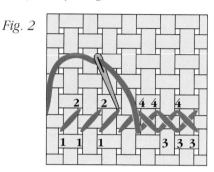

For vertical rows, complete each stitch as shown in Fig. 3.

Fig. 3

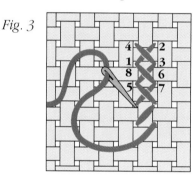

Embroidery Stitches

SATIN STITCH

Referring to Fig. 1, come up at odd numbers and go down at even numbers with the stitches touching but not overlapping.

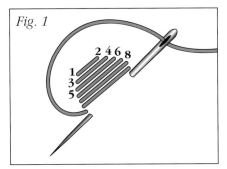

Fig. 1

STRAIGHT STITCH

Insert needle up and down in fabric as shown in Fig. 2. Stitch length may be varied as desired.

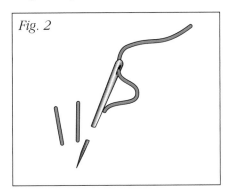

Fig. 2

LAZY DAISY STITCH

Bring needle up at 1 and go down at 2 to form a loop; bring needle up at 3, keeping thread below point of needle (Fig. 3).

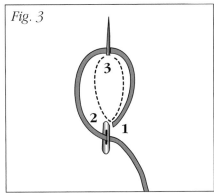

Fig. 3

Go down at 4 to anchor loop (Fig. 4).

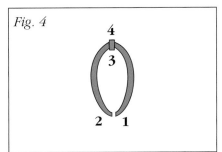

Fig. 4

BLANKET STITCH

Knot one end of floss. Push needle up from wrong side of garment, even with edge of appliqué. Insert needle into appliqué and then come up at edge again, keeping floss below point of needle. Continue stitching in same manner, keeping stitches even (Fig. 5).

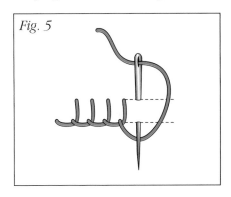

Fig. 5

RUNNING STITCH

Make a series of straight stitches with stitch length equal to the space between stitches (Fig. 6).

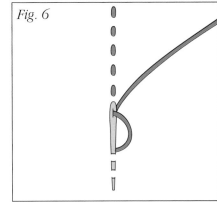

Fig. 6

KITCHEN TIPS

Measuring Ingredients

Liquid measuring cups have a rim above the measuring line to keep liquid ingredients from spilling. Nested measuring cups are used to measure dry ingredients, shortening, and peanut butter. Measuring spoons are used for measuring both dry and liquid ingredients.

To measure flour or granulated sugar: Spoon ingredient into nested measuring cup and level off with a knife. Do not pack down with spoon.

To measure confectioners sugar: Lightly spoon sugar into nested measuring cup and level off with a knife.

To measure brown sugar: Pack sugar into nested measuring cup and level off with a knife. Sugar should hold its shape when removed from cup.

To measure dry ingredients equaling less than $\frac{1}{4}$ cup: Dip measuring spoon into ingredient and level off with a knife.

To measure shortening or peanut butter: Pack ingredient firmly into nested measuring cup and level off with a knife.

To measure liquids: Use a liquid measuring cup placed on a flat surface. Pour ingredient into cup and check measuring line at eye level.

To measure honey or syrup: For an accurate measurement, lightly spray measuring cup or spoon with vegetable oil cooking spray before measuring so that liquid will release easily from cup or spoon.

Tests for Candy Making

To determine the correct temperature of cooked candy, use a candy thermometer and the cold water test. Before each use, check the accuracy of your candy thermometer by attaching it to the side of a small saucepan of water, making sure thermometer does not touch bottom of pan. Bring water to a boil. Thermometer should register 212 degrees in boiling water. If it does not, adjust the temperature range for each candy consistency accordingly.

When using a candy thermometer, insert thermometer into candy mixture, making sure thermometer does not touch bottom of pan. Read temperature at eye level. Cook candy to desired temperature range. Working quickly, drop about $\frac{1}{2}$ teaspoon of candy mixture into a cup of ice water. Use a fresh cup of water for each test. Use the following descriptions to determine if candy has reached the correct stage:

Soft-Ball Stage (234 to 240 degrees): Candy can be rolled into a soft ball in ice water but will flatten when removed from water.

Firm-Ball Stage (242 to 248 degrees): Candy can be rolled into a firm ball in ice water but will flatten if pressed when removed from water.

Hard-Ball Stage (250 to 268 degrees): Candy can be rolled into a hard ball in ice water and will remain hard when removed from water.

Soft-Crack Stage (270 to 290 degrees): Candy will form hard threads in ice water but will soften when removed from water.

Hard-Crack Stage (300 to 310 degrees): Candy will form brittle threads in ice water and will remain brittle when removed from water.

Softening Butter or Margarine

To soften 1 stick of butter, remove wrapper and place butter on a microwave-safe plate. Microwave on medium-low power (30%) 20 to 30 seconds.

Softening Cream Cheese

To soften cream cheese, remove wrapper and place cream cheese on a microwave-safe plate. Microwave on medium power (50%) 1 to $1\frac{1}{2}$ minutes for an 8-ounce package or 30 to 45 seconds for a 3-ounce package.

Shredding Cheese

To shred cheese easily, place wrapped cheese in freezer 10 to 20 minutes before shredding.

Toasting Nuts

To toast nuts, spread nuts on an ungreased baking sheet. Stirring occasionally, bake in a 350-degree oven 5 to 8 minutes or until nuts are slightly darker in color.

Preparing Citrus Fruit Zest

To remove the zest (colored outer portion of peel) from citrus fruits, use a fine grater or citrus zester, being careful not to grate bitter white portion of peel.

Toasting Coconut

To toast coconut, spread a thin layer of coconut on an ungreased baking sheet. Stirring occasionally, bake in a 350-degree oven 5 to 7 minutes or until lightly browned.

Melting Candy Coating

To melt candy coating, place chopped coating in top of a double boiler over hot, not boiling, water or in a heavy saucepan over low heat. Stir occasionally with a dry spoon until coating melts. Remove from heat and use for dipping as desired. To flavor candy coating, add a small amount of flavored oil. To thin, add a small amount of vegetable oil, but no water. If necessary, coating may be returned to heat to remelt.

Melting Chocolate

To melt chocolate, place chopped chocolate in top of a double boiler over hot, not boiling, water or in a heavy saucepan over low heat. Stir occasionally with a dry spoon until chocolate melts. Remove from heat and use as desired. If necessary, chocolate may be returned to heat to remelt.

Whipping Cream

For greatest volume, chill a glass bowl and beaters before beating whipping cream. In warm weather, place chilled bowl over ice while beating cream.

Substituting Herbs

To substitute fresh herbs for dried, use 1 tablespoon fresh chopped herbs for 1 teaspoon dried herbs.

Cutting Out Cookies

Place a piece of white paper or stencil plastic over pattern. Use a permanent felt-tip pen with fine point to trace pattern; cut out pattern. Place pattern on rolled-out dough and use a small sharp knife to cut out cookies. (*Note:* If dough is sticky, frequently dip knife into flour while cutting out cookies.)

EQUIVALENT MEASUREMENTS

1	tablespoon	=	3	teaspoons
⅛	cup (1 fluid ounce)	=	2	tablespoons
¼	cup (2 fluid ounces)	=	4	tablespoons
⅓	cup	=	5⅓	tablespoons
½	cup (4 fluid ounces)	=	8	tablespoons
¾	cup (6 fluid ounces)	=	12	tablespoons
1	cup (8 fluid ounces)	=	16	tablespoons or ½ pint
2	cups (16 fluid ounces)	=	1	pint
1	quart (32 fluid ounces)	=	2	pints
½	gallon (64 fluid ounces)	=	2	quarts
1	gallon (128 fluid ounces)	=	4	quarts

HELPFUL FOOD EQUIVALENTS

½	cup butter	=	1	stick butter
1	square baking chocolate	=	1	ounce chocolate
1	cup chocolate chips	=	6	ounces chocolate chips
2¼	cups packed brown sugar	=	1	pound brown sugar
3½	cups unsifted confectioners sugar	=	1	pound confectioners sugar
2	cups granulated sugar	=	1	pound granulated sugar
4	cups all-purpose flour	=	1	pound all-purpose flour
1	cup shredded cheese	=	4	ounces cheese
3	cups sliced carrots	=	1	pound carrots
½	cup chopped celery	=	1	rib celery
½	cup chopped onion	=	1	small onion
1	cup chopped green pepper	=	1	large green pepper

RECIPE INDEX

CREDITS

To the talented people who helped

in the creation of the projects in this book,

we extend a special word of thanks:

Mary Lee Braswell

Maryanna Brooke

Adrienne Davis

Catherine Fowler

Alicia Frazier

Alisa Jane Hyde

Laurie Knowles

Stephanie Roberts

Carol Tipton